Karma Finds the Chameleon

Donna J. Lehl

Aberdeen Bay

Albion - Harbin - Topeka - Washington, D.C.

Aberdeen Bay
Published by Aberdeen Bay, an imprint of Champion Writers.
www.aberdeenbay.com

PUBLISHER'S NOTE

Aberdeen Bay is not responsible for the accuracy of this book, including but not limited to events, people, dates, and locations.

International Standard Book Number
ISBN-13: 978-1-60830-062-4
ISBN-10: 1-60830-062-5

Printed in the United States of America.

ACKNOWLEDGMENTS

I am particularly grateful to Matty Kastel for giving me the gift of a story I felt compelled to write, to Hannah McCollum for encouraging me to write it, and to Ksenia Horobchenko for pruning and shaping my words without affecting my voice.

I also thank my children Heather and Jeremy for never saying "you're doing what?" and for becoming terrific adults and good friends, probably in spite of my influence. And I am immensely grateful for my father, Donald Dick, whose sometimes mixed messages included the one that has served me best – you can do anything you set your mind to do. But most of all I acknowledge that God is the source and I am but a channel.

Chapter One

The Funeral

I hadn't intended to make an entrance, but I found it hard to make myself get into the car and head for Hebrew Memorial Park, one of the three Jewish cemeteries situated in a half-mile square in an otherwise non-Jewish community. Long ago, after the closing of the bath houses in Mt. Clemens, most of the Jews had moved to the northwest side of Detroit. Now there wasn't even a synagogue in the county. And yet, within a mile of my house, there were these three Jewish cemeteries.

As we entered the main metal gates, I could see just to the left, behind the used car lot, a small group of people gathered under a rectangular tent. To reach them I had to drive halfway to the back of the cemetery, to the left fifty feet, then left again to double back to the section just to the north of the entrance. My daughter Heather and my three grandchildren were with me. We rode in silence until I could recognize some of the people who had gathered there and then, almost involuntarily, I started reciting the names of those who were there waiting for my arrival. I was surprised to see so many people from work, and surprised that some of those there cared at all. As soon as we got out of the car, we walked the few feet to the tent and took our places in the row of empty chairs next to the grave. Rabbi Shapiro looked at me expectantly and when I nodded in response, he began:

> And upon his conversion, he took a Hebrew name as is our custom. Steven took for himself the name Ze'ev ben Avrohom. When I

visited with Steven a couple of weeks ago in his home, I asked him about his choice of name. He looked at me with a glint in his eye. He curled his fingers in the way that we humans do when we want to portray the claw of an attacking animal and he said to me 'the wolf doesn't give up, it fights for what it believes in; that's me. I am a wolf.' He told me he was a descendant of the Cherokee Wolf clan. He loved animals, especially dogs and saw them as kindred spirits. Parenthetically, I will tell you that many Jewish children who are named Steven in English are given the name Ze'ev in Hebrew, so Steven somehow zeroed in on one of our society's current practices.

At the age of six, Steven contracted spinal meningitis and, although he survived the illness, it robbed him of his sense of hearing. And yet, Steven was a born fighter. Obstacles placed in his path only increased his sense that he was being challenged. Steven loved a challenge, so that if a challenge didn't present itself, he would seek it out. When I visited Steven in his home, I planned to spend a half hour or so and then off to my next call. He held me spellbound for a couple of hours, telling me the story of his life. I came out of that visit thinking what an interesting man! When I spoke to his wife Donna yesterday gathering information for this eulogy, she began her comments about him by saying—'Well, he was a very interesting man.'

The fully overcast, November sky suddenly became chillier and more saturated as a misty wind cut through the small group huddled near the open grave. I pulled my long black leather coat around me and moved a little closer to my youngest sister, Darla, who sat in the chair to my left. Heather, who was leaning on my right side, began weeping. I was surprised that she would mourn the loss of her stepfather, whom she had mostly tolerated for the eleven years we had been together. I had been a little uncomfortable that I could not work up any tears, but Heather's sobbing was about to make me break down. If I had known she would have taken his death so hard, I would have told her sooner. I knew I must tell her soon so she won't feel so bad. I swallowed hard as the Rabbi continued speaking:

> In his adult life, Steven told me that he was a commercial fisherman, a helicopter mechanic in Vietnam, a building contractor, a chef, a machinist, and a computer guru. He worked on the Alaska pipeline and he was the on-site manager of Donna's motel in northern Michigan.
>
> Steven was a seeker. He sought and learned his roots and talked expansively of his French and Indian bloodlines and his quest for a meaningful way to relate to his maker. This quest brought him to the study of many religions and finally to Judaism and the study of the Torah and the Tenusch. In his home were displayed Jewish books and ritual objects. He told me that he literally wore out several dozen copies of the Jewish Bible because it was his favorite reading material.

Oh brother, what a load of crap, I thought, trying not to show disdain for the Rabbi's words. I wished I could work up some tears or somehow act like a proper widow at my husband's funeral. I could feel the eyes of my friends and relatives boring a hole in the back of my head and I could almost hear them wondering why I did not appear to be grief stricken.

There were only a couple of people there who weren't somehow connected to me. Two women that I had never met were standing together near the back of the group. Since they were wearing yarmulkes, I presumed they were from the congregation where Steve had been converted. Was one of them Rabbi Karen? I felt a bit of remorse that I had blurted out to the Rabbi the reason for Steve's trips to Israel. I'm afraid I caused her to have less respect for him, which I don't think was my intent. She just caught me off guard, calling unexpectedly one afternoon while I was riding in the car with Hannah and her boyfriend Thad, after two days of court hearings in Grand Rapids. And since Hannah, my friend and confidant, was with me, it was easier and more compelling somehow, to blurt out the truth, a truth that would normally have remained buried in the recesses of an embarrassed and broken heart. The Rabbi's voice jolted me back to the present just in time to hear his conclusion:

> In the Jewish Tradition, we close with a few statements and thoughts which I will quote in Hebrew and translate into English. *Y'hey zichro boruch.* May his memory be blessed. *T'hey nishmoso trzerurah b'tzror hachayim.* May his soul be bound in the bond of eternal life.
>
> We will now lower the casket into the ground where Steven's body will hereafter rest. As is Jewish custom, his family and friends will now perform the final favor for their dear departed one by burying his earthly body.

The Rabbi picked up one of the four shovels poking out of the mound of dirt that had been removed sometime earlier from the hole into which the casket had now been lowered. He began throwing dirt upon the casket while praying, or speaking at least, in Hebrew. Some of the Jewish gatherers knew the ritual and stepped forward to do their part. Cha-thump, cha-thump, cha-thump. The shoveling took on a kind of rhythm. It appeared there was a sort of ritualistic four or five shovels of dirt to be thrown by each. And then, as instructed by the Rabbi, the shovels were to be returned to the mound for the next digger to retrieve and begin the burial anew. I wondered why the shovels weren't passed from one digger to the next. Wouldn't that be more polite? But what did I know? The rhythmic crunch of the shovel through the dirt followed by the thud of the dirt on the top of the casket provided an eerie beat—cha—thump, cha—thump, cha—thump, cha—thump.

Joel put down the shovel and my brother-in-law Bill picked it up. I was surprised to see Joel at the funeral. He was one of the partners at the firm where I worked. We had a pleasant but not particularly close relationship, so that he cared to attend was sort of gratifying. I remembered the time we were talking in the elevator one night on the way to the parking garage. He asked about Steve's trip to Israel after he had overheard me discussing it with another coworker. He said that he had attended school in Israel for a year when he was young. I asked if he had gone to the University of Jerusalem, which is where Steve had told me he was working on their computer system. Joel had a puzzled look as he replied that he had attended a university in Jerusalem, but that it was not named the University of Jerusalem.

Bill was the only member of my family who seemed to genuinely like Steve and he was certainly the only one that Steve liked in return. Most of the rest of the family either barely tolerated him or outright hated him. My father disliked him so much that he had tried to avoid our wedding, but at the last minute agreed to come because I was so upset. But Bill and Steve had a kind of closeness, a camaraderie that I had never seen between Steve and anyone else. Bill understood Steve's odd-sounding, deaf-person speech, and Steve could easily lip read Bill. He was the only one I knew who did not talk louder to Steve, as if hoping to somehow talk loud enough for him to hear. Instead, he carefully moved his lips, rarely making a sound audible to any nearby hearing persons. I remember Bill explaining that Steve had told him it was easier to read the lips of a whisperer than to read the lips of someone who was shouting—probably because the reader would be focusing on the facial expressions of the shouter, trying to determine just how mad he or she might be and the words themselves would be lost.

Bill acted like a man on a mission. He heaved huge shovelfuls of dirt into the hole. This was not the ritualistic four or five scoops, but probably 25, and yet he continued shoveling. The Rabbi, apparently concerned that some of these Goyim had misunderstood his command that they bury their friend, joked that there was a paid burial crew who would have to go home early if there was no work left for them to do. But his comment made no impression.

Darla, Bill's wife, joined him, shoveling with grim determination. Although she is tiny in stature, she is strong in spirit and on the end of a shovel. She later joked about the family's characteristic strong work ethic, saying:

"Don't tell a Dick to do something unless you want it done. And, it's best to get out of their way."

My youngest sister is the one most like me in temperament, despite the obvious differences in age and appearance. I was 13 when Darla was born and I moved out before my 18th birthday. Darla once commented that the only thing she could remember about living in the same household with me is that I wore a pink bathrobe and once, while cutting her hair, I nipped her ear.

Bill was working up a sweat now in the cold day that had turned misty:

"I bet Steve is laughing his ass off watching this," he mumbled.

The other mourners, if you can call them that, had mostly taken their turns with the two remaining shovels when I thought enough was enough. I signaled Darla to stop shoveling and I stepped forward to take her shovel. It was time for me to bury my husband. As I approached the remaining small mound of dirt, I gathered my thoughts for those worth remembering.

I wanted to remember the many women hurt by this man and I wanted to enlist their spirits to put him to rest. I vowed to throw a shovelful of dirt for each of them. Let's see, there was his mother, Kathryn, whom he heartlessly cut off from contact and whom I couldn't even find when he got sick to tell her that her son was dying. Cha-thump.

Next, the wives: Doris, with whom he had spent the most time, who he said had lied about her age and had stolen all of his belongings and sold them before he could divorce her. Cha-thump. Then there was Valerie. He didn't talk much about Valerie, except to say that she had daughters who had wrongly accused him of inappropriate touching of a sexual nature. God, I wonder now if it were true. He didn't seem like the type, but he would have been a lot younger then. As it turns out, he was not at all who he seemed to be. Cha-thump.

Then there was Susanna. He had claimed that she had gone to their apartment just after the entry of the divorce decree and taken everything she could get her hands on, leaving him with nothing. I talked with Susanna, who like Steve was deaf, by using the relay operator service that allows deaf and hearing persons to communicate by telephone, and I found her to be really sweet and sincere. I don't believe anything he said about her. This one's for you, Susanna. Cha-thump.

Then there was Matty—poor, sweet, Matty, even more gullible than me, or so I like to think. She was so shocked and devastated by the truth. She couldn't believe it was all a sham. I tried to help her through it all and in a funny way she helped me.

"This shovelful is for you, Matty," I whispered.

I knew I would e-mail her later that night to let her know that he was gone and that I mentally included her in the service. Cha-thump.

A few more shovelfuls for good measure. They could be for my sister Delma whom Steve treated like shit for no real reason and my friend Dawn who had supposedly been like a daughter to him and against whom he turned like a rattlesnake. I haven't talked to her for three years because of him. Her boys graduated without my recognition and congratulations. I need to talk to her, but I am just so embarrassed to admit that she was right and I was deluded. Cha-thump, cha-thump, cha-thump. I'm sure there were others. Cha-thump.

Chapter Two

The Telephone Call

My assistant Shirley was an old fashioned secretary, one who didn't take offense if I had a momentary lapse in political correctness and called her my secretary. She was older than me, I think, which is rare these days. She had been a legal secretary since before fax machines and computers and had all kinds of archaic skills. We got on well even though I was accustomed to doing most of my own word processing.

I didn't normally see her when I first came in because her cubicle was outside of an office several doors down from mine. But on that day, she was waiting for me outside my office door when I rounded the corner.

"Shirley, I'm in, but I can't stay too long today," I told her as I brushed past her and into my office.

"The doctor is supposed to meet with us to give us the results of the biopsy. I have to get out to the hospital by at least three o'clock or he'll just try to talk to Steve and then we won't know anything. I can't believe they don't try to get an interpreter to talk to a deaf man." I stopped to catch my breath and looked at Shirley, wondering for an instant why she had been waiting for me. But as quickly as the thought entered by brain, it left.

"I guess they don't have enough deaf patients to know how they are. And Steve always acts like he knows what you're saying, even when he has no clue. Anyway, I just want to return some calls, get through my mail and get that Quality settlement out, then I'm gone."

"Okay Chickie, let me know what I can do." She turned to walk away and then stopped and returned to the doorway, apparently remembering why she had come.

"Oh, you got a call from a foreign-sounding woman, but she wouldn't leave a message. I told her you should be in momentarily and you'd call her back, but she wouldn't leave her name or number. She said she'd call you back," said Shirley as she emptied the outbox and headed down the hall to her cubicle.

"Probably that French defendant," I mused as I recalled the last ridiculous call we shared—45 minutes while each of us searched for a word the other would understand. I had to keep fighting the urge to speak Spanish, the only foreign language that I had any familiarity with. It was hard enough to try to explain to the owner of a small business that you sued them because you wanted them to return money that the now-defunct debtor paid them for goods they had shipped to the debtor, much less explaining the intricacies of bankruptcy law to someone who spoke another language. I had a lot to do and not much time, so I knew I had to settle down.

A few hours later, after answering my e-mail and snail mail and drafting the settlement agreement, I thought about heading out to the hospital. I knew I still needed to make a couple of phone calls before I could leave and I thought about grabbing a sandwich on the way because it was sure to be a long night.

I knew the news wouldn't be good. The articles on the Internet described in brutal straightforwardness the course of pancreatic cancer. There was only one type that allowed a surgical solution that could provide some possibility of remission. Otherwise the treatment was only palliative – for pain relief – and the average longevity was just three to five months after diagnosis. I had sort of mentally prepared myself for what the doctor was about to say, but I had never let on to Steve what I suspected and what I had learned about the disease.

"Beep"

"Damn, I'll never get out of here," I said aloud. "Maybe I should just let it go to voice mail so I can finish up in time."

"Beep," the phone insisted.

Of course, it could be the doctor or the hospital, I thought. "Donna Lehl," I said crisply into the phone.

"Hello? Is this Donna Lehl?" It was a tiny, foreign-sounding, tentative voice.

Why the hell don't people listen when they call someone? You say your name and then they ask you if you are who you just told them you are.

"Yes, this is Donna Lehl." I tried to keep the impatience out of my voice. "How may I help you?"

"This is Matty from Israel. I am calling to find out how Steven is. I haven't heard from him in nearly two weeks. He told me he was not well and that he may be going to hospital and that he may require a surgery. I am so worried about him and I decided to try calling you because he told me about you and I thought surely you would know how he is and if he is still in hospital."

"Yes, he's in the hospital and he's not well. He's been there for about ten days and they've been doing tests and he had surgery to open a blocked bile duct, so he's feeling a little better, but. . . ."

"I hope you don't mind me calling you like this, at work and all, but when he was here he told me that you were his best friend and I know that he depends upon you, and I found one of your business cards in his belongings and I asked him about it, so I knew you were a lawyer in Michigan. I was just so worried and I thought I just had to call you to learn how he is."

"Wait a minute!" It took a few minutes for her words to sink in. "Let's go back to 'I'm Matty from Israel.'"

"Yes, I am Matty Kastel. Steven came to see me in Israel a few months ago."

"Okay, but Steve told me that his friend Matty in Israel had a wife named Sarah and a couple of kids and a brother named Joseph who also had a wife named Sarah, but you sound like a woman, not a man." My face was hot and my voice was getting louder and starting to shake.

"Forgive me if you are a man and my ears are playing tricks on me" I said, gaining a bit more composure.

There was a long pause from the other end of the line. "No, I am a woman. I can't imagine why Steven would tell you that I'm a man. I do have children and a brother named Joseph and a sister-in-law named Sarah, but I'm certainly no man." I could hear the confusion in her voice.

Kay, one of the partners and a law school friend who was instrumental in my hiring, appeared in the door. After asking the caller to "hold on a minute," and conscious of my red face, I cupped my hand over the phone. "Can I come see you after I finish with this?" I asked, trying to keep my voice steady.

"Of course," Kay replied, out of sight as soon as the words left her mouth.

"So, is it a tumor? Will he be all right? Will he be getting out of hospital soon?" Matty fired questions at me. "I knew that you would know how he is because he told me what good friends you are."

What had been a flush became a full-fledged throbbing, like the top of my head was literally about to explode. "Lady," I spat out, "I'm not just Steven's friend, I'm his wife!"

Silence, or near silence, followed. It was what they call a pregnant pause, a full, extended period void of talking, but full of breathing. Funny how even being separated by thousands of miles and connected only by wires and fiber optics (whatever they are) still allowed me to hear her breathing, sharp little bursts of air, like someone having a panic attack and badly in need of a paper bag.

Shirley appeared in the doorway then and gently eased the door shut. Oh shit, I thought, I hope John didn't hear me. All I need is for the office manager to suspect I have more problems than just a terminally ill husband.

"He told me he was never married," shrieked Matty, after apparently regaining the ability to speak. "I asked him many times because I thought it odd that a man could get to be his age and never be married and he always swore that he hadn't been married. How long have you been married?"

"It's been almost eight years that we've been married, but we've been together for more than eleven years." The highlights and lowlights of those years came back to me and felt like I imagined the experience of having your life flash before your eyes in the moment before what is sure to be your demise. "I took my time deciding because I was concerned about being wife number four."

"Four!" Matty fell silent again.

"If you don't mind telling me, what kind of relationship have you had with Steve?" I asked her, putting my hand across my forehead to still the throbbing. "Is it romantic?"

"Why yes, we've been talking about getting married, once he's permanently retired from the military and is able to obtain his Israeli citizenship. I've had some friends tell me that I should be slow and cautious and I had a pre-marriage agreement drawn up and gave it to him to review with his lawyer."

"You have got to be kidding me!" I involuntarily slapped my forehead as if that would somehow make this conversation sensible. "How long have you known him?"

"We have been together two and a half years. Well not really physically together except for his two visits, but we have talked online almost every day for two and a half years and we met to see if our love was real and we spent every day of his visits together, except for a few days that I had to go into work."

It was my turn for silence. I replayed the intricate stories he had told me, not once, but built up layer upon layer, month after month, in the way that normal things occur, not all at once, but in increments, the way life unfolds. First he described his lively discussions with the Jewish people he met online. That led to his interest in their religious beliefs, which led to a chat room where learned rabbis discussed the Torah, which led to his interest in converting, and later brought encouragement for him to engage in rabbinical studies in Israel. And his first trip there, last year, was paid for by his friends and their friends so that he could come and work on their computer systems. I thought that seemed logical enough since he was really good with computers and had worked for EDS as a hardware specialist.

"So let me see if I've got this right." I said. "When he came to Israel in April, he didn't stay at the University of Jerusalem and take entrance tests for rabbinical school?"

"No, he stayed with me, every day and every night and did not go to any university."

"And the first time he came there, did he work on computers for the university and for some businesses?" I asked while aimlessly making boxes around boxes on the legal pad on my desk. It was starting to feel a little like a deposition. "Did a group of people pay his way for these trips?"

"Well, I'm not sure where he got the money for the most recent trip, but he sent me a thousand dollars American and I purchased the ticket and sent it to him. The first ticket I paid for myself because he said that Dee, the woman he lived with, had control of his military pension and took it all for his care. I sort of felt sorry for him. He worked on my computer a little bit, but I don't think he touched anyone else's computer."

"Okay, so he told you he had a friend named Donna and

he lived with someone named Dee?"

"Yes, when he got out of the military, he said he needed to be reacclimated to civilian life, so the government placed him at Dee's home and she received his pension and rarely gave him any of the money, and he worked for her at her motel. She was mean and greedy and they were constantly arguing and he was trying to figure out how to get away from her." Matty spoke quickly, words spilling into each other. "And he told me that you were his only real friend in Tawas and that you listened to him and always tried to help him. He was very upset when you had to go to work in another city and he didn't get to see you very often."

"Jesus, I had to go to work in the city because he always refused to do anything to support us and I lost everything I had trying to run that motel and practice law in Tawas. This is just too crazy!" I said, dropping the pen from my hand. Later, after replaying the conversation several times in my head, I came to think that both "Dee" and "Donna" were me depending on how he felt about me at the moment. Of course, there was always the possibility he was just a skilled liar.

"Matty, I don't blame you," I said. "I think we're both victims of his deception, but, I need to go to the hospital because the doctor is supposed to talk to us this afternoon and give us his diagnosis. And I have to think about what to do about this. I may want to talk to you again about some things, do you mind if I e-mail you?"

"Of course, I am sure I will have questions for you too once this all sinks in and I want to know about his health, if you don't mind?"

"Sure, let's exchange e-mail addresses and I'll let you know what the doctor has to say. I've got to go, Matty." I said again, more urgently. "I'm sure there are some folks here wondering what's going on in here and I really don't want my sordid story to be the topic of conversation around here. Bye."

"Good-bye and I'm really sorry."

"Yeah, me too."

I was shaking as I replaced the receiver in the cradle. I don't know how long I sat staring at the bookcase across the room or really just staring in the direction of the bookcase. My eyes and thoughts were really focused on the past eleven years, not in any kind of organized way, but in a series of unrelated images and a cacophony of sounds both joyful and anguished, smells, ranging from disgusting to comforting and feelings running the gambit from fiercely affectionate to utter despair. I hated roller coasters. I hated the feeling of being out of control. If I ever thought I was in control of my life, I was just fooling myself. I wanted to kill the son of a bitch.

Shirley was knocking gently on the door. "Can I come in?"

"Yeah, what's up?" I said, trying to sound nonchalant.

"Are you all right? Do you want to talk about it?" Her voice was tentative. "I could tell that something was wrong, that's why I shut your door."

"Yeah, I suppose everyone who was nearby could tell." I said and let out a big sigh. "I'll have to talk to Kay, since she was in the door long enough to tell something was going on."

"So are you going to tell me or not?" Shirley asked as she closed the door again and sat in the shabby client chair between the door and the bookcase.

"Well, you are my secretary and the origin of the word "secretary" comes from Latin for one who holds confidences, and I don't want my personal life to be the stuff of rumors in this place, so if I tell you this, you will have to swear not to discuss it with anyone, ever—knowing, of course, that if this ever comes back to me, I'll have to kill you!" I said looking at her with a forced grim expression. She looked back like she was trying to get a reading on my seriousness.

"Of course I won't discuss it with anyone." Shirley

chuckled a little nervously, knowing that while I loved to joke, I was probably only partly joking and partly deadly serious.

I repeated the substance of the telephone call to Shirley, in large part trying to impress upon myself the reality of what I never could have imagined an hour before. Looking back, it is really amazing how a single incident, a few moments in time, can change everything that you believe, how you think and feel. Strange how time is measured from such a moment, how life is different after the call from what it had been before. Like the assassination of JFK and the attack on the twin towers of the World Trade Center, the telephone call from Matty Kastel on July 28, 2004, is forever etched in my mind and soul. I will always remember the date, where I was, who I talked to about it and the feelings I had, even though they defied description. That call changed everything.

"So what are you going to do?"

"I don't know. What can I do? I said shaking my head slightly. "He's dying. I can't leave him to take care of himself. And now that his girlfriend knows about me, she won't be taking care of him. He has no one but me. I am pissed off, though. If he wasn't dying, I'd probably want to kill him. How could I have been so fucking stupid not to have known?"

"Well, don't be too hard on yourself; he is obviously a very good liar. Just think of all the crazy things he told her and she believed him."

"Yeah, I guess so. Maybe on some level I knew. Actually, I did suspect at one time that he was romancing someone online, but I never put two and two together to connect the online romance to the trips to Israel."

I remembered the office he reluctantly shared with the motel business. He begrudgingly allowed the credit card machine, cash box, business records and paraphernalia to be in "his office," but he constantly bemoaned his lack of privacy. And then there was the love poem in his handwriting that he didn't give to me. Also, the keyboard tray that faced the corner opposite the door that proved unsuitable. He said the light bounced off the computer screen. So he moved it so that the door would be in his peripheral vision when he looked at the screen. Well, apparently he still felt that I could sneak up on him and read what he was typing, so he moved it again to the portion of the U-shaped desk that directly faced the door. What a fool I was. I just thought he didn't want to get caught telling his friends what a bitch his wife was. I never guessed he was talking several hours every day to his girlfriend.

"Are you going to confront him?" Shirley's voice interrupted my thoughts.

"Oh yes. I think I have to." I smiled slightly at Shirley. "I don't think I could play the loving little wife. I'm pretty transparent. And he knows how to read me. He'll know something is up the minute I walk into the room. I sure don't know what I'll say to him though. I can't believe how he's made my life into a fucking soap opera!"

"Well, my unsolicited advice is stay married so he'll have your insurance, visit him in the hospital if you must." Shirley looked directly at me, enunciating her words like someone who knew what she was talking about. "But if I were you, I wouldn't take the bastard home. If he ever gets out of the hospital, send him to a nursing home."

"He's probably lucky he married me, not you." I laughed. "I don't feel like being around him, but I can't see myself kicking him out in his condition. I think I have to take care of him."

I pushed the chair back from the desk. "I've got to get going, the doctor could be stopping by Steve's room anytime now. Tell Hannah I'll call her from the road and don't tell her or anyone else about this."

"Okay, okay, wild horses couldn't drag it out of me." Shirley scurried out my door and made room for me to fly through it. "Just be careful driving to the hospital, please."

"Yeah, yeah," I said, letting her know I appreciated her concern. "I'll see you tomorrow if I'm not locked up for assaulting my hospitalized, critically-ill husband."

Somehow I got to my car and drove the 13 miles from downtown to the hospital. I don't remember thinking about anything, but I must have been doing something during the 20-minute drive. Thinking was a natural thing to be doing while driving, but looking back now, I can't remember what, if anything, I had been thinking. The trip felt unreal, like I was watching myself go through the required motions, but couldn't really feel myself doing them. I felt strangely detached and sort of numb.

Arriving at Beaumont, I slammed the car door, walked briskly through the parking structure, then down the pedestrian tunnel to the hospital and on to the south elevator bank. The door opened as soon as I pushed the Up button. Thank God I'm alone, I thought since I really didn't feel like smiling and exchanging small talk with anyone. I leaned against the wall of the elevator and closed my eyes, wishing I could melt into the drab green paint. My respite from the rest of the world was short lived as the bell rang, signaling the arrival of the elevator and the opening of the door.

I stepped out of the elevator on the seventh floor and automatically rounded the corner to the right. The sights, sounds and smells of the nephrology/oncology ward were now familiar. Although numb, I was still painfully aware of my surroundings. The smell of Pine-Sol and overly processed hospital food wafted through the air. Empty wheelchairs, patients with half-opened gowns pushing IV stands, abandoned mop buckets, and patients on transports all had to be navigated. And the sounds were never ending – silverware dropping, feet shuffling, wheels turning, and the overhead PA system barking – "Dr. Sharma, call 7231; all available personnel to room 7108, stat; housekeeping, please report to room 7131."

Steve's room was almost at the end of the oncology ward. As I drew closer, I could feel my pace involuntarily becoming slower. God, what AM I going to say to him? Maybe that is the point. God, please direct my mouth, I prayed silently as I turned to enter his room.

"Oh, there you are my love." Steve said, his face lighting up as I entered the room. "I was beginning to worry about you. I've missed you so much" he said, while reaching toward me with his right hand and forming the "I love you" sign with his left.

"Yeah, right!" I said sharply.

He seemed to immediately identify that something was wrong, probably because I stopped at the foot of his bed instead of coming to the side where he could reach me and pull me toward him for a kiss. I didn't even want him to touch me.

"What's wrong, honey, did you have a bad day at work?"

"Yes, I had a very bad day. I found out today that my husband has been cheating on me for the last two and a half years." I looked right at him and spoke slowly and enunciated the words carefully. I wanted to make sure he understood me and that he would register the severity of the situation. His eyes flashed a kind of fear, or shock maybe, and he opened his mouth and looked as though he was about to protest what I had just said.

"Don't you DARE deny it!" I practically shouted, although I was trying to be quiet. "I've had enough of your lies! I talked to Matty on the phone today for about an hour. I know all about your visits, your daily conversations with her and your plans to leave me and return to Israel to marry her." My hands curled into fists wrapped around my handbag handle. "You lied to me and you lied to her and I will never believe another fucking word you say."

A nurse drifted into the room with a syringe. If you want a nurse, nothing will bring one. If you want a few minutes of privacy, they miraculously appear. I forced a smile and unclenched my hands.

"How are you today?"

"I'm well, thank you, and how are you?"

"I'm fine. Steve's had kind of a bad day. He's been anxious, wanting me to call you to see what time you would be here, complaining of a lot of pain. We're trying something different, but it makes him nod off, so once I give this to him, he'll probably fall asleep for awhile." She injected the medicine into the IV, fluffed his pillow, wrote in his chart, and rustled out of the room.

"Honey, come here. Please sit by me." Steve said, stretching out his hand. "I am so sorry to have hurt you." He continued when I didn't respond. "I don't want to be with her. I have been trying to break it off. She knew I was married. I don't know what I was thinking." He paused, looking at me for what I imagined was some softening on my face. "You know it happened when things were not going well between us. Remember I said I was going to leave you because that is what you seemed to want? But things have changed and I know now that I really love you and only you. Please, come here."

I wanted to scream or throw something, but of course I could do neither. I could feel the adrenaline really pumping by then, so that my careful enunciation was impaired by my shaking lips.

"I don't believe she knew you were married. I don't believe you intended to cut it off and I don't believe you love me. I understand that people make mistakes and I could forgive you for becoming interested in someone else, but I don't know if I can forgive you for lying to me every single day for the last two and a half years. And, even if I can ever forgive you, I will never believe you or trust you again. Never!" Fear flashed in his eyes, like an animal caught in a cage when it first realizes it can't get out.

I had to take a breather then because I felt like I was about to scream or grab him and shake him. I began again, a little more controlled. "Don't worry. I'll take care of you because I made a vow that I would. But please don't expect me to hug and kiss you like this never happened. This is the worst day of my life and I don't feel like touching you."

He hung his head down in silence. As I looked away from him, I was still shaking, but not crying. Where were the tears, I wondered. I looked back at his now scrawny body as if it would yield answers to the questions that were burning in my brain. Steve closed his eyes and, as the nurse had predicted, nodded off.

Dr. Newman, the head of the oncology department, suddenly appeared in the door. I immediately knew this was a bad sign. If the test results were good, one of his young associates would be around as usual. But if the head of the department showed up, it was probably because the news was the worst.

"How are you today" he perfunctorily asked as he held out his hand to me. "And how is Mr. DeVore feeling? Are they controlling his pain?"

"Yes, the nurse just gave him something for the pain." I said, as I prepared myself for what was to come. "I'm afraid he's not alert enough to talk with you."

"Well, that's alright." He said, sounding mildly irritated as he looked over my shoulder at Steve, as if checking to see if he really was sleeping. "I'll talk with you first, then I'll check him out and see if I can talk with him. If not, I'll come back tomorrow and talk with him then. Let's step out in the hall, shall we?"

As soon as we got out of the room, I noticed my Uncle Henry walking down the hall toward us.

"Hey kiddo, how're you doing?" He asked quietly as he approached. I was really grateful that he arrived, especially when he did. I immediately felt his emotional support.

"I'm okay. Doc, this is my Uncle Henry. This is Dr. Newman, Steve's oncologist."

The two men shook hands, and then Dr. Newman started talking in a low and solemn voice. "As you know, we did a biopsy of the liver and the pancreas. We took samples in seven locations and we've received the results back from the lab. I'm afraid that the samples confirm that your husband does indeed have pancreatic cancer." Henry let out a small but audible groan beside me. He didn't know that this was what I had expected, so he wasn't prepared for the diagnosis.

"So what is the treatment? I asked. "Can you do a Whipple Procedure?"

The doctor looked a little surprised at the question. "Are you a nurse?"

"No, I'm a lawyer, but I've been reading for months about pancreatic cancer, because that was my fear when the doctors started telling him there was something going on in the pancreas."

"I'm afraid his cancer is not operable." He said matter-of-factly. "The care that we can give him is palliative. It is a terminal illness, however, we will do everything we can to manage his pain." He patted my shoulder in his first demonstration of empathy. "We'll release him as soon as we determine what type and dosage of pain medication is most effective and I would like him to take a type of chemotherapy called Gemzar. It is tolerated well by most patients and should help to reduce the lesions, which should help to reduce the pain. I'd like him to take a dose before he goes home."

"Okay, well," I said hesitatingly, still trying to take in all that Dr. Newman had said. "I will talk with him about this when he's able. I expect that he will do whatever you recommend, as long as the pain of the treatment isn't worse than the pain of the disease. When do you think he can go home and what kind of care will he need there? Can he be left alone while I work or will I need to stay with him?" I shot questions at him, wanting to get them all answered before he could decide he needed to move on to the next patient.

"I'm not sure" he said, answering some question, but I wasn't sure which one. I wished I had not asked all my questions in one breath.

"He still has a lot of pain. Maybe we can do something surgically for the pain." He said, as if thinking out loud. "He shouldn't be left alone the way he is now, but we should be able to get him feeling better before we let him go home. I want to talk with Dr. Gaines, the gastroenterologist to see if there are other things we can do to make him feel better during the time he has remaining."

"How long does he have?" asked Henry, apparently finding his voice after a long period of silence.

It was obvious the doctor didn't like the question and was carefully considering his answer. "It depends on so many things, I really can't guess," he said. "Let's just see how he recovers from the biopsy, and if the chemo shrinks the lesions. Do you have any other questions?" He asked, while looking down at his watch. He suddenly seemed anxious to be somewhere else.

I know how he feels, I thought. I wanted to be somewhere else too, with a different reality.

We returned to Steve's room and Dr. Newman quickly looked at his chart, listened to his chest and took his leave. Henry and I found chairs and made small talk for a while as Steve continued sleeping fitfully. When it became clear that Steve would not be waking up soon, Henry excused himself.

It was nice of him to come, I thought, especially since he had recently been hospitalized with congestive heart failure and lived an hour and a half away. He was the only one of my relatives to visit him at the hospital. Of course, Steve had not endeared himself to my family.

Dad and Steve barely tolerated one another. Steve was openly hostile toward my sister Delma, on account of some minor incident which hurt my feelings, but which I had long since forgotten. With the rest of the family, he shared a sort of polite recognition, except that after eleven years together, he still confused my brothers' names. I tried to remember that he had never actually heard their names pronounced and that Dana and Darrell might have been similar enough to be read the same on the lips. But a part of me believed he mixed up their names because he just didn't give a damn.

As soon as I was sure that Henry had gone, I checked to see that Steve was still sleeping, and then slipped out of the hospital room. I felt I just had to escape. I couldn't bear to look at him and I didn't want to touch him or even talk to him anymore that day. But I couldn't go home either. Perhaps I could get Hannah to go out for a few drinks. I knew I could use a few drinks and I needed to tell her about Matty because she was my best friend at work and I had already told Shirley and Kay. That's it, I thought, only those three will know about this at work. I trusted they could all keep quiet and no one else needed to know.

I paid the valet, climbed into my car, which had been retrieved by another young man and started toward the east side of the city. Then I dialed the cell phone. It rang once or twice.

"Hello," Hannah said, obviously recognizing my number on her phone. "What's up?"

"You want to go out for a drink or two or three?"

"What's wrong—bad news at the hospital?" She asked, sounding concerned.

"I'll tell you when I see you, but I think I need a drink to actually tell the story."

"Well," Hannah said tentatively. "Thad is cooking a pork loin and we'll just throw on some more vegetables if you'll come eat with us, and we've got some scotch for you."

"I don't know," I hesitated. "I was only planning to tell this to you, no one else."

I had never met Thad, but I had heard a lot about him from Hannah. They had been dating for years but had only recently moved in together. They met at U of M law school and after graduation they had a mostly long-distance relationship with her in Chicago and him in Muskegon, then she moved to Detroit. I really did not want to meet him tonight and I really didn't want anyone else to know about this, at least until I could process it myself.

"Thad can keep a secret or, if you prefer, we can tie him up in the basement." I laughed at the thought and responded. "It seems a little cruel to eat his dinner and then tie him up" I said. "Even I am not that mean. I guess if he cares to listen, I'll tell him too, but warn him I'll have to kill him if he ever repeats the story I'm about to tell."

"Now I'm really curious," Hannah said, her tone serious. "Where are you?'

"Not far, I'll be there in about 10 minutes. Later."

I flipped the phone shut and shoved it back into my purse.

"Fuck, I still can't believe it," I said aloud.

But, I knew it was true. Yesterday life was challenging, but seemed real. Now it seemed so unreal. What was really bizarre was that I had thought my life with Steve had been real. I guess he just had another reality.

There on the right were the 1950s, red-brick townhouse apartments where Hannah and Thad lived. I turned in the drive and tried to identify Hannah's door. Hmm, there's her car, I thought, but nothing else looks familiar. I had been here once before, but hadn't memorized the house number or exact location. I pulled into the one remaining parking spot and as I did, a door opened and there was Hannah's smiling face and behind her, and a full foot above her face, appeared the smiling, bespectacled face of a young man with scraggly blond hair and a scruffy beard. So, that was Thad. He didn't look ten years older than her.

Before I could lock my car door and walk across the driveway, Hannah began the introductions. "Hey, you got here quick. Donna, this is Thad. Thad, this is my friend Donna."

"Hannah tells me you can use a drink," Thad said, shooting me a quick smile. "What would you like? I've got some scotch and I just went out for some soda because Hannah said that is your preferred drink."

"That would be just fine, thanks Thad."

After everyone got their drinks, we discussed the difference between soda water and tonic because Thad had bought tonic thinking it was soda and I had been shocked by the unusual concoction. Then we engaged in a little chit chat about the apartment and what it was like for them to finally be living together after a three-year long-distance relationship. Hannah apparently could stand it no longer.

"So, what happened?" She said, leaning forward. "Is it Steve? What did the doctor say?

"He has cancer and it will kill him, but I knew that before the doctor told me." I said, considering how to transition to the rest of the story. "But what I didn't know is that he's been having an affair for the last two and a half years with a woman in Israel."

"You're kidding!" Hannah shouted, nearly tipping over the glass she had been reaching for. "How did you find out?"

"She called me. His mistress, Matty, called me." I automatically made the phone to the ear sign with my right hand. "She was worried about him and called me because she knew I was his friend."

I retold the story of the phone call, as much to let the reality of it sink in as to explain to Hannah and Thad what had happened. It seemed a little more real each time I retold the story.

"I used to think my life was pretty normal," I said. "Now I feel like I'm living in a fucking soap opera!"

"Oh no, you've gone way past soap opera into the realm of the Jerry Springer Show," Hannah said, leading me to images of chair throwing and confrontations with baby daddies. "I can't believe that bastard!" Hannah finally exclaimed. Thad shifted uncomfortably in his chair.

Although I appreciated Hannah's indignation, I was feeling the need to try out the idea that had been half-formed in my brain for the past couple of hours.

"I think this is an example of karma," I said, slowly choosing my words. "He'd been using me and he'd been using her and he lied to both of us. Maybe he really was just a con man and when he felt I was losing patience with him living off of me, he found himself another mark. But now his abuse of others had come around—you know 'what goes around comes around'." Hannah and Thad sat patiently listening; letting me organize my newly formed thoughts. This is why her friendship meant so much to me, I thought. And Thad was pretty rare for a guy.

"And now he's dying in a most unpleasant way." I continued, shaking my head. "If I was losing my husband to cancer, believing that the love of my life was being taken from me too soon, I would be devastated. And, if I'd learned about his affair when he was healthy, I might have been so angry with him that I would have wanted to kill him. But to learn of his infidelity at the same I find out that he's dying sort of softens the blow of either awful event." I took a drink of my scotch and tonic as Thad excused himself to start putting dishes in the dishwasher in the next room.

"One thing is for sure, I don't need to punish him because his punishment has been meted out by a higher power. I will mourn his death less because he's already left me. What really amazes me at this moment is the difference that a day can make in a life."

Hannah nodded somberly before adding "you got that right."

The scotch provided clarity, but only for a little while. Soon it would cloud my judgment and dull my senses. I knew I had to go home before I became too dull to drive.

I helped carry out the last of the dishes and glasses and we made a little small talk about the next day at work. When the last of the dishes were loaded, I hugged Hannah, waved goodbye to Thad and quickly made my exit.

God, what a day, I thought as I circled the apartment building, looking for a driveway to the street.

Chapter Three

The Matty Chronicles

I couldn't wait to get home so I could e-mail Matty and continue our conversation. I hoped she'd been serious when she said she wanted to know how Steven was doing and that she welcomed any other questions I might have.

When I arrived at the little apartment I had rented to be near work, I first walked the dogs, who were unaccustomed to being cooped up all day alone. They were a pair of Pembroke Welsh Corgis who spent nearly every day that we had them nestled at Steve's feet. First we got Kodi, the male, when he was about six months old. We were still living on Lake St. Clair and Steve was home alone every day while I worked. He wanted Kodi to act as a hearing dog and he was pretty good at indicating when the phone or doorbell sounded or when the oven or microwave bell rang. He adored Steve and went everywhere with him. He bit anyone who smacked Steve, even playfully. He had nipped me a few times, but always looked very remorseful, as if he had just realized what he'd done. As he got older, Steve began talking about how he needed another young Corgi to take over Kodi's duties and wouldn't it be fun to get a puppy, with a little warm belly, this time.

We got Andouille a few months after we got married. She had a name before she was born because Steve always called Kodi a fat little sausage and being fans of New Orleans and Cajun food, we thought it would be funny to name a dog after the famous spicy sausage indigenous to the area. When we picked her from the litter, she was a tiny handful of fur with big stand-up ears. Her registered name was Sunrise Side Spicy Andouille, but we mostly just called her Dooie. Even though she spent most of her days with Steve too, she was my dog.

When I let the dogs out, they took turns herding each other for a while and I took the opportunity to watch them and to laugh at their antics, letting my mind rest from the emotional turmoil of the day. They tried to make friends with the young miniature pinscher who lived in the next unit, but he was territorially guarding his patch of lawn, so I directed Kodi and Andouille to another area. Eventually they did their business. After a short walk I took them inside and gave each of them a treat and some praise.

I poured myself a scotch and soda and fired up the computer. It was really late for me to be up on a work night, but I was way too wired to think about sleeping. I just wanted to know more about this woman who lured away my husband and I was curious about the other person Steve had become with this woman. I thought about asking all of the questions that were burning in my brain, and then I started writing, not sure where the thoughts would lead.

From: Donna Lehl
Sent: Thursday, July 29, 2004 12:22 AM
To: 'Matty '
Subject: Steven De Vore

Matty,

I'm sorry we "met" under such unpleasant circumstances. To follow-up on my promise to let you know about Steven's health, the doctors have confirmed the worst—he has inoperable pancreatic cancer – a particularly aggressive form. I don't know what options he will choose for dealing with it, but I will help him decide what will be best for him. I confronted him on his deception of both of us and he owned up to some of the facts, admitted he was wrong, but in a roundabout way suggested I was to blame. He also said you were aware that he was married. I don't believe that and I cannot believe anything he says, especially if he has anything at all to gain. I told him you did not want to have any more to do with him and he said that is what he wanted too. I will pray for you and for Steven. God knows I need all the help and direction I can get for dealing with the situation I have found myself in.

Donna

I hoped that Matty would respond, but I really wouldn't have blamed her if she just deleted the message and tried to get on with her life. Yesterday she was worried about her boyfriend because she hadn't heard from him for 10 days after they had spent hours online almost every day for two and half years. Today she knows that the man she was considering making a life with already has another life with another woman. And besides that, he was very ill and she would probably never see him alive again. That's a lot for anyone to absorb in one day. But I expected Matty to reply. I thought she must have at least as many questions as I did. Finally I turned off the computer, got ready for bed and somehow managed to find sleep — no doubt the result of utter exhaustion.

Morning came. I anxiously checked my e-mail, but there was no response. I went to work for a few hours, keeping mostly to myself so that I would get enough work done so I could leave early to get to the hospital in time for Dr. Newman's visit.

Dr. Newman came as he promised and he bluntly told

Steve that he had inoperable cancer of the pancreas and that all that medicine could do for him was help relieve his pain. They call it palliative care. From his head nodding and smiling, I could tell Steve really hadn't understood. Dr. Newman asked him if he had any questions and Steve shook his head and said "no." He looked at me with eyes that said I would have to explain later what he didn't understand. I was angry because the sign language interpreter that I had requested had not come before the doctor arrived. I didn't want to be the one to explain to Steve his grim future. When the doctor finished, Steve grasped his right hand in that two-hand style that was supposed to convey congeniality and gave it an extended shake.

As soon as the doctor left, he looked at me and raised his hands, signing "what" then "say." I had to tell him again what the doctor had tried to communicate. I delivered the news slowly looking him in the eyes so he could read my lips, but lacking any appearance of compassion. I was acting merely as an interpreter. He had cancer. There was no cure. They could give him chemo, but it would only help the pain and delay the inevitable. He was going to die. I knew he understood my words, but I didn't think he really accepted them as his reality, because he showed little emotion. He motioned for me to take his hand and I reluctantly complied.

We sat quietly for a while. We did not speak of Matty or the conversation of the day before, but it was there in the room like the elephant everyone refuses to recognize. He held my hand uncomfortably tightly, only loosening his grip when he fell asleep. I took his slumber as my opportunity to escape. I was so tired. I just needed to go home and get some sleep.

But before I could sleep, I had to check my e-mail. There it was—Matty's reply.

From: Matty
Sent: Thursday, July 29, 2004 12:13 PM

To: Donna Lehl
Subject: Steven De Vore

Dear Donna,

Thank you for your prompt reply in regard to my phone call to you yesterday (28th July, 2004). I too am very sorry to have "met" under such unpleasant circumstances. Although we spoke for some time on the phone, my head was reeling under the shock of all the things you told me about Steven, and though I appreciate your time and honesty to all my questions I asked you, there are still so many questions left unasked which I need answers to, if you can answer them at all. I see you as a friend in need, in my troubled time.

Most importantly, in reply to one of your statements that you mentioned in your e-mail about the fact that Steven said I was aware that he was married, is totally untrue (probably another one of his never ending lies). He adamantly told me that he had NEVER been married, nor had he ever had any romantic relationships with other women, because of his impairment (his deafness). Even if I had known that he was married, I would have ended the relationship, because it is not in my nature to have affairs with married men.

I know there is a certain limit to what I can write in an msn message, so if in case this is too long, I will send it to you in 2 parts.

These are the main questions I would like answers to:

1) The two times that he came to Israel

(one being on my expense) he pressed and encouraged me to have a closer relationship, with the ulterior motive of eventually getting married. Although I was not convinced to get married, I said I would think about it, and even prepared a contract, similar to a pre-nuptial contract which he took back with him to review.

2) My concern also, is that he may be lying and deceiving other women, which we are both unaware of.

3) Part of his life story that he told me was that he had served in the military for about 30 years as a secret agent, and in my naiveté, I believed all that he told me, although sometimes I would question him about it, there were some things he could not give me answers to as he was "sworn under oath" not to say anything, and I took his word at face value. (I couldn't understand the fact that seeing he was deaf how the military could employ him at all as an agent, and yet he had convincing answers to everything).

4) I'm also curious to know, does he have any children from all 4 of his marriages? (That you know about?)

5) The last question for now – how he was able to deceive you, and if it had not been for my phone call, maybe you would still be kept in the dark. Were you ever aware that he lied to you too, during your marriage?

Obviously there are many more questions that are still open between us. I'm sure you feel as I do now – very much confused and under shock. I want you to feel free to e-mail me if you have any questions that you would like to ask me, and I'm prepared to answer anything you would like to know.

I hope you do take the time out to answer me, since my heart is bleeding inside and your reply will maybe, somehow, make it easier for me to know the answers – WHY?

Donna, you too will be in my prayers, and hope we both get the guidance that we surely need.

Matty

I laughed uncontrollably for several minutes when I read the part about Steve being in the military. He was totally deaf. He could not be admitted. He told me that he'd wanted to enlist and when no branch of service would take him, he said he went to Vietnam as a civilian helicopter repairman. That probably wasn't true either. He would have needed training and he had never talked about getting any. Where and when would he have had such training?

But now, one sort of strange incident suddenly made some sense. One day about two years ago, before I'd moved to the city to work, he asked me if I would take a picture of him against the background of Lake Huron, so he could send it to his friend Matt in Israel. He said he wanted to show Matt that Lake Huron was so big it looked like the ocean. I took the picture as he requested, enjoying the opportunity to practice with my new digital camera.

It was kind of cool outside, but I was a little puzzled that he went to the closet to get his fully lined, camouflage hunting jacket. He wanted only the open water in view, not the park across the street and not Tawas Point.

"Just get me from the waist up," he directed.

I framed the picture with the sun across his face and Tawas Bay in the background. I avoided Gateway Park so that the background would be nothing but water. When he looked at the picture I had taken in the viewer, he demanded that I take another because I had not done what he told me to do. I had gotten his jean-clad legs in the photo.

"I told you, just the waist up," he said in disgust and resumed his pose.

"What difference does it make?" I remembered yelling, irritated with him, as I framed the shot again. "What the hell difference does it make if your legs are in the photo?" I took the best picture I could, using the maximum zoom and remembered thinking I could crop off his legs later if he didn't want them.

At the time I didn't think any more about it, but now I think that the picture was designed to make Matty think he was in military uniform. It makes sense since American soldiers are seen on television all over the world in camouflage fatigues. She would have thought his stories of military life were true if he resembled the soldiers she was accustomed to seeing on the news. The blue jeans covering his legs would have ruined the image. And was the lake supposed to be some ocean in the background?

Pretty funny, I thought, that I had taken pictures of him to send to his girlfriend. And that wasn't the only time. Once, when he was particularly proud of his weight loss, he put on the pants he had worn for our wedding and held out the waist revealing an opening that would accommodate another small person. I took his picture and printed him a copy so he could send it to his friend Matt to demonstrate his dieting success. I had been happy to comply because I was proud of his success, too. I had designed the diet for him and had prepared all of his meals. I sort of acted as his personal nutritionist.

How *was* he so able to deceive me?

There were countless times that he told me things I found

hard to believe, but I guess I had trained myself to be too open-minded. For my whole adult life I had been a student of the human psyche. My undergraduate majors had been sociology and psychology, and my work had always been with people at their worst. First I had been a social worker who specialized in juvenile delinquency, child abuse and neglect, and then as a lawyer, a large part of my career had been handling the legal issues of the same constituency. I had learned that the truth was often stranger than fiction. But it was more than that. Now I realized that he was a *really* convincing liar. He was a pro. He knew how to weave the truth with the fiction to create a believable whole story.

Although I had some questions of my own for Matty, I felt obliged to answer the ones Matty had asked first. I poured a drink and settled down to answer her e-mail.

From: Donna Lehl
Sent: Friday, July 30, 2004 12:09 AM
To: 'Matty '
Subject: Steven De Vore

Hi Matty,

Funny that you feel the need to ask me additional questions, since I too have felt that I wished I had asked you certain things that I now have questions about. I feel like we are kindred spirits of sorts. I am trying hard not to think that we are a couple of really stupid women and trying to view us as loving and trusting people who are so honest we find it hard to believe that others would treat us any differently.

Please understand that when Steve told me that he had told you he was married, I didn't believe it for a minute. You sounded too shocked on the phone yesterday to make it up unless you are a professional actress. And, I could see in his eyes how desperate he was to have me believe that it started innocently enough and just got out of hand.

I'll answer your questions first, and then ask what is on my mind.

As far as I know he never served in the military and it stands to reason because he would never be accepted in the US Armed Forces because of his deafness. He told me he was a civil servant helicopter mechanic in Vietnam, but I have never seen any documentary evidence of this. As I understand it, his early years were spent in an orphanage; he lost his hearing while living there when he was about 7 years old and I have heard him tell doctors that he lost his hearing to spinal meningitis, flu type B, which included a very high fever that also made him sterile. To my knowledge he has no biological children. He has talked of stepdaughters that he has had in the past and I have two grown children. He has told me that he was married three times before we got married in 1996, that is what he wrote on our marriage license and I have seen some divorce papers. He was never too long without a wife. He has told me horrible (and sort of unbelievable) stories about some of his ex-wives — shot his dog, sold all of his possessions, etc. Probably all lies to invoke my sympathy.

He did work for EDS (I have seen papers, info on stock plan, deferred retirement, etc.). He got fired and I felt sorry for him (we were dating at the time) and I invited him to move to my home.

He wanted me to marry him right away, but I put him off for three years. He worked in computer hardware I think, but I have also heard him talk about working in computer crime. I wondered about that, but didn't have any evidence it was not true. Before EDS he apparently worked for GM as a machinist. In his younger days he claimed he was a chef (I took this to mean he was a cook), worked as a commercial fisherman and on the Alaska Pipeline.

He probably would have continued deceiving me if you had not called. I suspected a couple of years ago that he was having an Internet relationship (harmless enough I thought) because (1) he was online for hours every day – claimed to be working, but he never made any money and he always seemed to be laughing and having such a good time (2) he turned his computer around from where it was designed to be so I could not walk up behind him and see what he was typing (not that I would intentionally snoop), and (3) I once found a love poem on his desk while looking for something for my motel business – but of course he denied what it was, said it was only his attempt at creativity. I figured he was lying when he vehemently denied that he was doing anything other than talking to his friends, but I could not prove anything and he always made it appear that I was wrong for suggesting there was anything amiss.

I think he was able to deceive me because if I didn't just go along with anything he said he would accuse me of being a bitch, trying to start trouble, not being willing to allow him to have a life, blaming me for putting him down. He would say to me all of the things he would express about his fictional "Dee."

If there are or were other women, they were probably online, or they may be associated with his conversion to Judaism. He would go to the Shul or to classes without me, of course, but other than that and the two trips to Israel, he was rarely away from our home and until last September, I worked at home.

Now my questions for you: This is pretty indelicate, but I need to know because of his "impotence" for the last six or seven years. Did you have a physical sexual relationship with him? Please forgive me for invading your privacy by asking such a personal question, but he has claimed he could not have sex with me because his diabetes caused erectile dysfunction. If that is not true, it is probably the most hurtful lie he has ever told me.

When he came to Israel the first time, did he work on computers for schools, businesses or otherwise? Did he stay anywhere besides with you when he came there? Is there a Joseph, and two Sarahs, do you have any children, did he dine with your extended family or is everything he told me about his trips there a lie? This year, did he stay in a dormitory at the University of Jerusalem? Was he being evaluated to go to rabbinical school there? Did he convert to Judaism for you (as far as you know)? Who paid for the trip you did not pay for?

Finally, did he give you any jewelry? Specifically missing is an amethyst ring in gold, and a year 2000 pendant that disappeared about the time he received the gold Star of David necklace (probably from you).

Thank you for your prayers, Matty. You have mine as well. I am confident that we will both find comfort and happiness in our lives because, despite this weird connection now between us, we will be blessed by the lessons our lives teach us.

Regards,
Donna

It was just after midnight when I clicked "send" and powered off the computer. I got ready for bed and barely remembered my head hitting the pillow. I was grateful for the exhaustion that kept me from thinking anymore about Steve and Matty.

The next day was like many days that were to come. I got up, got ready for work, walked the dogs, went to work for a few hours, went to the hospital for a few hours, came home, walked the dogs, warmed up a TV dinner and then sat down to the computer to check my e-mail. I hoped there was a message from Matty, but at the same time, I dreaded reading what she would say.

Sure enough, there was another message.

From: Matty
Sent: Friday, July 30, 2004 3:58 PM
To: Donna
Subject: Steven De Vore

Hi Donna,

I'm happy to answer any questions you have despite the fact we are both under sorry circumstances, because I feel that he too has hurt you very deeply to your very soul. His deceit has left me devastated and betrayed, since I have been so honest and open with him from the very beginning, but indeed try not to think what fools he made of the both of us. We are just innocent victims caught in Steven's web of lies and deceit.

Now to answer your questions in the order you have asked me. Again, please feel free to ask me anything you want, and I will be totally honest with you, though my replies will probably hurt you even more, which I apologise for in advance.

Yes, we did have a very active sexual relationship nearly every day and the sex was wonderful, despite the fact, that yes, there were times in the middle of our love-making he was unable to perform as usual. He told me he was taking some form of medication to increase his libido.

When he came to Israel the first time he in no way worked on computers for schools, business or otherwise. On the both times he came here he was living with me in my home and never stayed in a dormitory at the University of Jerusalem. No, he was not being evaluated to go to rabbinical school here (as far as I know, unless he was being evaluated by his rabbi in Detroit that I have no knowledge of). He did express an interest in furthering his studies though. As for converting to Judaism, I in the beginning told him that I did not care one way or the other if he did convert or not, but because his eventual intention was to come and to stay in Israel with me, it seemed best for him to live as a Jew. It turns out in the end according to Israeli and Jewish law, he would have had to convert to stay, but aside from that, he always expressed an interest in Judaism and to becoming Jewish anyway. I admired him for that fact, and was happy and easier for me that he still wanted to become Jewish.

No, I do not know of any Joseph or two Sarah's though I do have a cousin called Sarah, whom he briefly met. Yes, he did dine with my extended family and did meet up again briefly with all my aunts, uncles and cousins here, as well as meeting up with my mom and brother on a number of occasions.

Yes, I do have 2 teenage children, two girls, one of whom is serving in the army, and the other is at high school.

The second trip Steven paid for himself. He told me he was doing odd jobs for the people there (computer work, mowing lawns, shoveling snow, etc.) and that was how he was able to earn a few dollars, since according to him, this fictional "Dee" was receiving all his pension pay that he was supposedly getting from the military during the time he spent in "her home." He claimed that he was almost penniless, and by doing odd jobs, he was able to save for his trip. He sent me the money for his second trip, because all the flight arrangements were made from here, since he said it was cheaper to get tickets in Israel, which I sent to him via air mail.

As for the jewelry that he sent, you are indeed correct in your suspicions. I first received the year 2000 pendant in the first year of our relationship and later that same year he sent me an amethyst ring in gold, telling me that it was to be my engagement ring. At the same time he also sent me another much older looking ring which he said was his mother's wedding ring. These of course I will send back to you, at the address you choose to give me. The gold Star of David, I did send to him 2 years ago for his birthday.

Finally, what I wanted to add, was that I spent a lot of money on Steven while he was here, which put a financial strain on me, but I didn't mind at all, since all I wanted was for him to have a good time and to enjoy himself while here. I felt sorry for him for the kind of life he was living while with "Dee." We went on numerous trips, staying at a hotel and at a log cabin, which was all paid for by me. Going grocery shopping, often going out for dinner or drinks, again all paid for by me, but I must admit that here and there, he would offer to pay on occasion.

When he was here the first time he bought me a watch, and the second time he bought me a perfume, besides a few other gifts that he brought with him, and I bought him gifts too while he was here. Of course we exchanged parcels many times during our relationship. He would send me things from the U.S. and I would send him items of food and clothing from here. I have all the greeting cards we exchanged with each other. Yes, he also did write me love poems.

Donna, while he was here, we really spent the most wonderful times together. He treated me and made me feel like a queen. We were like 2 honeymooners, hardly spending time away from each other, except on one or two occasions when I had to go back to work for a few days. During those times he would either be working on and updating my computer, tidying the house and cooking great meals for us. He too told me he was a chef, and we often exchanged recipes.

He entered my home and my heart, he met my friends and family, and though I believed he was single and despite his impairment I believed in him and all he said, like someone who is blind when in love (which I surely was!).

I was put under pressure from all sides to separate from Steven at the time we started the relationship, but he insisted I be strong and encouraged me to do what I thought was right for the both of us. I was very much in love with him, and did not want to listen to all the warnings, because his attitude towards me was very warm and loving. He made me feel wanted and cared for. There was a time when I too planned to come see Steven in the U.S. but he seemed to dissuade me from doing that.

Donna, was he at all surprised when you told him I managed to make contact with you? What do you think we should do now since our conversation and e-mail exchanges about Steven, to try and understand and to make head or tail of what happened here, and how he managed to deceive both of us? I haven't stopped crying, am unable to sleep and feel very restless. I wake up with tears every morning and go to sleep with tears every night. I'm still so very hurt and confused.

Please let me know what the doctors say about his condition and if they have any estimate regarding how much time or how long they think he has to live. How long will he be hospitalized for? I assume if the cancer is that bad and inoperable, there would be no sense for him to go through with the unpleasant procedure of chemotherapy.

I know I said earlier that I do not want any further contact with him, but on second thoughts, if it's still possible, I would still want one more time to chat with him and try to understand what happened and what reason he had for going through all this charade, just for my peace of mind.

Although I feel very much betrayed by Steven, I still wish him well for both your sakes.

Be strong Donna, in these very difficult times you are living under now. My thoughts are with you.

Matty

I felt nauseated as though poisoned by the anger, hatred, disbelief and feelings of abandonment that welled up within. Without the aid of sleep or drugs, I felt assaulted by flashing visions of him lying with this other woman, enjoying intimate touching and intercourse leading to satisfying orgasms – all while I had been sadly unsatisfied. There had been hundreds of times over the past several years that I had attempted to engage in normal marital intimacy with him only to be pushed away and gently told:

"I can't do it, it doesn't work. I'm sorry; it's the diabetes and the medicine. It has made me not fully a man."

I had begged him to try Viagra or the newer Cialis and even went so far as to ask his doctor to write him a prescription. The doctor gave him a sample supply of the little blue pill and Steve gave it a try one time. It worked, but he didn't seem at all happy about it. He acted as though the sensitivity was painful and complained of a blinding headache. He could not be convinced to use it again, although he did allow the doctor to test his blood for its testosterone level. It was below normal levels and the doctor had prescribed medication in a patch, which Steve used only sporadically.

It became painfully clear that he really did not want to have intimate contact with me. I had been angry at times, depressed at times, and sometimes I just tried not to think about it. He made me feel like I was abnormal and insensitive not to understand that it hurt and shamed him more than it could possibly matter to me. He couldn't do it. How could I not understand?

And now here was the truth—he was only impotent with me. I could hardly catch my breath. I felt as though there was a boulder on my chest. I wanted to scream, to cry, to let it out, but I had forced the feelings so deep inside, I could not reach them to set them free. I kept going back to the same place in Matty's letter hoping it would trigger something so I could just feel again. It didn't.

Funny, for all of my inability to feel anything about what was most important to me, I was absolutely furious about the jewelry and about what I now suspected had been other thefts. The amethyst ring had begun as a gift from a coworker at Schafer & Weiner, the small bankruptcy firm I had worked at before I left to buy the motel and start a new life on the shores of Lake Huron. Sybil had gone to Thailand and when she returned, she gave me the beautiful dark-purple oval stone in a little, yellow oriental pouch. I was surprised because I didn't feel that we were close enough friends for such a lovely gift, but Sybil had explained that she knew I would appreciate the stone because she knew I loved beautiful jewelry.

It took several months of looking, but I finally found a setting that I liked and I had the stone mounted in a heavy gold ring. Steve had shopped with me and took an active part in finding just the right setting to showcase what was probably the most saturated amethyst I had ever seen. It was breathtakingly purple. Steve liked to say that he had bought the ring for me, but in truth, I had used my own credit card to pay for it, and of course, I had paid the credit card bill too.

I'd owned the ring for probably six or seven years when one day I went to my jewelry box to get it and couldn't find it. I didn't think too much about it that day because I had a habit of taking off my jewelry in various places – the kitchen, the bathroom – or while cleaning motel rooms. Sometimes I'd lay them down or put them in a pocket. But over the next several months I had looked everywhere I could think of, including behind and under all of the furniture. I was afraid that my cat Girlfriend had found it and had played with it because it was a small shiny object, much to a cat's liking. One day Steve walked in on me while I was lying on the floor dragging a yardstick across the bedroom carpet under each piece of furniture that had an opening.

"What in the world are you doing?" he asked.

I sat up and turned around to face him so he could read my lips. "I lost my amethyst ring and I'm determined to find it," I said. "I bet Girlfriend knocked it off the dresser and then pushed it under something."

"When did you have it last?" he asked, sounding for all the world as though he was trying to help me remember where it might be.

"I can't even remember. I've been looking for it for months. I didn't say anything because I figured I'd find it and I didn't want you to think that I can't keep track of my things even though it sometimes seems that I can't."

"I'm sorry, let me help you. I know it's hard for you to get down on the floor with your arthritis."

He took the stick from me, helped me up off the floor and set about dragging the stick carefully under the dresser, his chest-of-drawers, and the two night stands. He even got the flashlight and looked behind the pedestal bed in case it was in the space between the pedestal and the wall.

He was not successful and now I knew why. He had sent my ring to Israel to be Matty's engagement ring.

And he had also given her the gold 2000 year pendant I had bought him for Christmas/Hanukkah in 1999. He proudly wore it for a while, probably six months, and then it was gone. He said he had lost it while mowing the lawn and had looked for it but never found it. So there it was – the truth. I was married to a liar and a thief! And there was no doubt in my mind that I had probably paid his way to Israel this past spring as well. I thought he should have made more money renting rooms than he did, even if he had missed half of the customers because he couldn't hear them ringing the doorbell. He had pocketed all of the cash sales, just as the prior owner had bragged that he had done.

Even though I felt betrayed and used, I felt even sorrier for Matty. She thought this was the man of her dreams and he probably never told her the truth about anything. There was likely a huge void in her life since she used to spend hours every day talking to him online. She was almost certainly anxiously awaiting my reply. I poured myself a glass of wine, then returned to the computer and began writing.

From: Donna Lehl
Sent: Friday, July 30, 2004 9:15 PM
To: 'Matty '
Subject: Steven De Vore

Thanks Matty, for giving me what I asked for – information. But you are absolutely correct, knowing the truth hurts me more than I thought I was capable of hurting. Asking you about this stuff and getting answers was a little like picking a scab and making it bleed, just as it was beginning to heal a little bit. Please don't feel too bad about the money you wasted on Steve, I supported him for the last 11 years except for his disability checks that until recently he contributed to our expenses because we just spent more money than I could make and he would never work. I paid all his bills, even gave him a $20 here and there to just do with as he pleased which is probably where he got the money for the plane ticket, unless he stole from me in some other way I have yet to determine.

The year 2000 pendant I gave him as a Hanukkah (or Christmas) gift (I can't remember which). He proudly wore it until one day it just "got lost." I thought it was weird because it was on a very strong chain. You are welcome to keep it if you can stomach looking at it. As for me, I can no longer wear my wedding rings because they seem to represent a sham.

The amethyst ring is the only thing you have that I would really like back. A coworker of mine brought the stone back from Thailand and gave it to me and I had it set. Steve helped me choose the setting and always said he gave me the ring although I paid the bill with my own money, so I really bought it for myself. The wedding ring he gave you might have been his mother's, or maybe stolen from someone else. It was not mine, unless it is white gold and lacking a stone. If that is the case, it may be the ring from my first marriage; I guess if that is the case I might like to give it to my children someday.

You know what is really ironic about some of the gifts he gave you? They often came from me. I made wine charms for his friends "Matty & Sarah" and "Joseph & Sarah." I insisted he take gifts to Matty and Joseph and their families when he went to visit and even made suggestions: the state quarter coin sets, trinkets for the girls. When he would assemble boxes of American foods or spices, I probably bought and paid for them. I did wonder though about the many gifts he received from you and the cost of the postage was pretty excessive for a casual friendship. He often used our joint credit card for postage and then I paid the bill.

Matty, if you want to have contact with him, you are welcome to him. I have no further romantic interest in him. I only feel an obligation to take care of a now very sick man that God brought into my life for whatever lessons I needed to learn. It is a little surreal that he developed terminal cancer and at the same time I learned about this horrible deception. If he had been well, I would have had the divorce papers drawn, filed and served before the end of the day of our first contact and I would have seen to it that he left as penniless as he arrived. If he had died this horrible death without me knowing about this aspect of his life, I am sure I would have felt a terrible loss. But the way that things have developed, I feel some compassion for him, but I had no guilt at all in confronting him, even knowing that he was dying, and I also feel that it will be a relief for me when he finally does pass on. Somehow this makes his dying easier for me.

What I am most struggling with at this point is that he does not want to make decisions regarding his care. He wants me to make them. A part of me wants him out of my life as soon as possible, but my ethics tell me that I have an obligation to do what is best for him. The doctors won't really say how long he has to live, but the impression I get is that without treatment he may live six to eight months. If he has treatment, it could be twice as long or longer. But the doctors are not impressed with his progress (or lack of it). He requires more pain medication than they expect he should and he doesn't eat what a bird might. He has lost probably 50 pounds in three months. He will be in the hospital until at least the beginning of next week, because his pain is not managed and he isn't eating. I guess when he is released I will bring him to my apartment, but I cannot stand the thought of ever sleeping in the same bed with him again. Perhaps I can convince him that he needs a hospital bed in the living room.

What would be really interesting would be for the three of us to have a meeting. Then he couldn't lie about either one of us or the circumstances. It would be a sort of "intervention" for the chronic liar. If you would be inclined to come here for that purpose, I will do what I can to help you arrange it. And maybe we should invite his rabbi too because I think there is some deception there that needs purging; I just haven't figured out what yet. If you choose not to do that I would understand completely.

If you are inclined to send me my amethyst ring, send it to the address at the bottom of this message.

Matty, I am beginning to feel like we are sisters – soul sisters – as American black women often refer to themselves. Perhaps that is the reason for this weird connection that we have.

Best Regards,
Donna

I shut down the computer, took the dogs out for their last walk of the day, and took a long soaking shower. While I readied myself for bed, I downed the last of the bottle of wine I had opened when I came home from the hospital. The wine had not dulled the pain, which was a pain without description or location. I supposed that this condition is what is commonly referred to as malaise.

I went to bed, but did not sleep, not all night. I prayed a lot – for Matty, for myself, and for Steve and anyone else who ever felt such total bewilderment.

The next day was Saturday. When I got to the hospital, Steve was alert and anxious to see me. He smiled weakly and held out his arms beckoning me to come to him. He knew me so well, I thought. In the past, no matter how angry I had been with him, I could not stay mad. Usually, by the next morning I was over whatever had been my problem the day before. But this was different. I wasn't over his deception and perhaps I never would be. But there were some things I needed to get off my chest. I needed to tell him how I felt about what Matty had told me. It would be one of our last discussions concerning his infidelity.

During that visit I confronted him about the theft of my ring, about his plan to marry Matty and stay in Israel and about his feigned impotence. At first he tried to protest and then he seemed to accept that I wasn't buying what he was saying. Eventually, he was reduced to tears which made it unlikely that he could read my lips anymore. While I spewed venom, I had no concern for his feelings, health or future. I just needed to get it out. Finally, the purging was over. I felt as though our marriage was over, but like it or not, our lives were still intertwined. I would be there through his illness and to help him die. I would make the best of it. What else could I do?

I spent most of the day there with him. I took him to the shower down the hall and bathed him, because he refused to let any of the female nurses see him naked. He hadn't minded showing himself to Matty, I thought. But of course that was about 50 pounds ago, before the skin on his legs, stomach and butt began to drape in folds like old-fashioned living room curtains. His penis had even retreated under a bag of skin, kind of like a shy turtle head. I could hardly stand to look at him and when he caught sight of himself in a mirror, horror crossed his face before the tears welled up in his eyes. I tried to distract him from the image of himself with cheerful talk and general busyness. "Okay, turn around so I can scrub your back. Now we need to rinse the soap out from under your arms so you don't break out in a rash," I said. "Let me put a towel down so you won't slip on the tile."

Mostly I was just talking to myself because he wasn't looking at me. I swaddled him in the fresh towels I'd carried in and helped him dress. He grabbed my arm with a hand I no longer recognized the feel of. His once rough, lawn-mowing, gardening, dock-repairing hands were soft and smooth as a baby's hands might be. How could ten days in the hospital make such a difference?

"I love you so, darling." He said weakly.

"Yeah, right," I replied, almost automatically. It was to become the substance of most of our future conversations. Did he mean it? Probably not. He was just afraid to die alone. His dependence was familiar. I remembered the early days of our relationship. Whenever I went off somewhere alone, I would return to find him pacing in front of the house, anxiously looking down the road from where I had come. He had said to me literally hundreds of times: "I thought you left me." I couldn't really understand that kind of insecurity, but I had made it my life's work to make him feel more secure.

This was going to sound crazy, but I married him after three years of holding out because I thought that then he would feel secure in my love for him. For a smart woman (or so I thought), with degrees in sociology and psychology, I had been remarkably naïve when it came to my own emotional life and my understanding of the man I had chosen to take to bed and to heart, for better or for worse.

We really had loved one another and he frequently displayed affection, unlike my first husband, Ron. I remembered thinking once, shortly before I told Steve I wanted to marry him – he's not perfect, kind of mean and kind of lazy, but he is the only one I know who will love me forever, no matter what. Boy, had I been mistaken!

I got him back to bed, tried to get him to eat the lunch they had brought him and then watched him sleep for a while after the nurse gave him a shot of morphine. I took his slumber as an opportunity to slip out, get some lunch, walk about the hospital, and clear my head. When I returned he was awake and had that same old "I thought you abandoned me" look on his face.

"I thought you had gone home," he said. "I'm sorry I can't stay awake, honey."

I thought about the way he always misspelled honey —"H U N N Y." Sometimes his inability to spell annoyed me, but usually I found it endearing, and thought it was part of his charm.

"No problem" I said. "It's the drugs."

His dinner was delivered and once again he ate one or two bites of the main course, a taste of the canned fruit, and then sipped the coffee until it became cold. The food was awful because he had told them he only wanted kosher foods. Strange, I thought, since he had never been able to eat truly kosher in Tawas. Kosher hospital foods were prepackaged, over processed, shelf-stable meals and Beaumont Hospital only had three choices, which they rotated. I tried a bite of one during another visit and couldn't understand how anyone could eat it.

"Steve, you need to give up the kosher food. God will understand," I urged. "You need to take in some nourishment and you can't seem to choke down that stuff." Besides, he was Reform not Conservative or Orthodox, I thought. But he would hear nothing of it. He also would not eat.

When he became more alert, but before the pain kicked in again, I made him walk down the hall and back a few times. On the far end of the hall, I bought him a Vernors ginger ale and sat with him in the lounge while he drank most of it and rested. On the way back to his room he showed signs of fatigue, leaning more heavily upon my shoulder and walking ever more slowly. I worried I had bitten off more than I could chew and may not be able to get him back. I was grateful when he made it back to his bed.

"How're my dogs? Do they miss me?" he asked.

"Of course they miss you. Kodi sits by the window all day looking for you." He smiled as he nodded off again. I didn't know if Kodi really looked for him, but it made him feel better to think he did. I waved to the nurses as I made my escape.

After I got home, I walked the dogs, fed them and quickly ate a microwaved dinner. I fired up the computer and opened my e-mail. There it was — today's installment from Matty.

From: Matty
Sent Saturday, July 31, 2004 4:40 PM
To: Donna
Subject: Steven De Vore

Hi Donna,

You have no idea how bad I feel about the fact that Steven was so underhanded about stealing the 2000 year pendant and amethyst ring from you, and that he used your credit card in order to purchase and pay for all the goods he bought and sent me at your expense. So besides lying and being deceitful, you can add to his characteristics that he is a scoundrel and manipulative person, taking advantage of both of us once again.

The wine charms he also sent me, but the state quarter coin sets he distributed to my ex-husband, and I can't remember to whom else he gave the other sets.

I admire you for the fact that you still feel an obligation to still take care of Steven, but I suppose after 11 years of knowing, living and being married to a person the feelings of compassion just don't disappear that completely. Believe it or not, I too feel sorry for him at this time, despite all the hurt, betrayal and anger I feel inside. I have such mixed feelings at the moment... at one time I am wishing him to be in hell, and at another moment, I remember all the wonderful times we spent together... do those times mean absolutely nothing to him? Does he not have a tiny bit of conscience within his being? Does he feel no regrets or remorse? A million and one questions are revolving in my head, with no sensible answers. I sometimes feel I am going crazy.

I sympathize with you in your decision regarding Steven's care. It's a difficult choice to know what to do, but despite it all, I suppose what really counts from now on is the quality of life and not the quantity. The future holds a great burden for you ... it will not be easy for you to take care of a person with cancer, and knowing that little by little he's dying each day. I'm sorry if I sound callous, but that is the reality of life, which I'm sure the doctors have confirmed anyway. Steven was telling me in the last month of how much pain he was suffering and that how, lately, it was getting more and more difficult for him to keep his food down. I already suspected the worst, but did not want to confirm it to him till I knew for sure the results of the biopsy. The last time I saw Steven he was not looking at all well, and my heart went out to him.

Donna, you gave me the suggestion of setting up a meeting between the three of us, and

I thank you for your offer to help me arrange for it. I've started thinking about this, and I'm sorely tempted to come, just to see the reaction on his face when he sees me, and to look deeply in his eyes to see if I can fathom what his thoughts really are. If I do decide to come, it'll probably be sometime next year during the spring time (and if he's still alive by then). If and when I do decide to come, I will of course let you know. I'm sure too that his rabbi will be just as amazed if she has to learn about the real facts about Steven.

You are right Donna when you say that we are like kindred spirits, or soul sisters, because in a strange way that is how I feel too. I guess it's because we are in the same boat, and each suffering in our own ways just because of Steven.

Donna, I will try and forward the jewelry to you as soon as possible, together with the wine charms, and of course, will let you know beforehand when I do send it so you know when more or less you can expect it.

If you have any further questions from me, please don't hesitate to ask me, and I hope I can do the same too.

I'd appreciate anyway being posted about Steven's condition, whenever you have the time to let me know.

Best regards,
Matty

I was tired, but I didn't want to disappoint Matty. These daily messages were important to me. I imagined they were equally important to Matty. They seemed to have a sort of therapeutic value. I guess it was just nice knowing that I was not the only stupid woman to be so clueless about Steve's deception. Somehow it felt better knowing that I was not the only ignorant one in the triangle. Another example of the adage – misery loves company.

> From: Donna Lehl
> Sent: Saturday, July 31, 2004 9:51 PM
> To: 'Matty '
> Subject: Steven De Vore
>
> Hey Matty,
>
> I hope you are feeling a little better tonight. I was so upset when I read your last e-mail (last night) that I forgot to eat dinner, then I downed a bottle of wine. Ouch, what a headache I had to go along with my heartache. But I am better today. Strangely enough it helps me to see Steven and to confront him with additional information. It's sort of like torturing him. And he's too weak to fight back, but that doesn't keep him from continuing to lie. I'm afraid he's a pathological liar.
>
> Please keep the wine charms – I made them for you (of course I thought you were Sarah, Matty's wife) but they were intended to be my small gift to Steve's Israeli friends. And as far as I am concerned, the 2000 year pendant is yours too. I gave it to Steve as a gift and if he wanted to give it to you, that was his right. Taking that amethyst ring was another story. And I think you almost got my wedding set too because I was getting ready to leave one

Sunday to go back to work and I wasn't wearing my rings because my hands were swollen, so I handed them to him and asked him to put them in the front pocket of my suitcase along with my watch. Well, I got back and the watch was there, but my wedding set wasn't. I e-mailed him right away and asked him about my rings. He made up some story about how he must have missed the pocket because he found the cat playing with them on the floor. I may never wear them again, but I paid for them, so I want them.

I think I figured out how he got the money to come to Israel the last time. He's been running the motel by himself, so any time someone paid in cash, he probably pocketed the money, cleaned the room, and told me he had no business all week. I thought business was down more than I had anticipated. Of course I'll never know for sure and I doubt he'll ever admit anything if he is not caught red-handed.

He is now scheduled for a liver biopsy on Monday. The doctor told me that if the cancer has metastasized in the liver, he will not be offered radiation, just chemo. They continue to increase the dose of painkillers, but still he has pain. He's not eating enough to nourish a bird. I don't know if they will send him home after the test on Monday or not. I'll keep you posted as to his condition, but it may be from my work computer once I get him home. I can guarantee you he will be snooping on my computer.

Matty, please only send my amethyst ring, keep anything else he gave you. If you send it in a smaller box, like the size of a box of checks, it will fit in my mailbox and there should be no problem with me getting it.

Take care of yourself and I will try to do the same.

Warm Regards,
Donna

Matty must have been waiting for my message because the morning brought her reply. I read it with my morning coffee before going to the hospital.

From: Matty
Sent: Sunday, August 01, 2004 2:59 AM
To: Donna
Subject: Steven De Vore

Hi there Donna,

I don't know if I'm feeling a little better, all I know is that it will take me a long time to come to terms with myself regarding this business with Steven. I still feel in such a turmoil about it all, but I thank you for your good wishes. I can imagine that you must be feeling in the same position as I am at the moment, and it's a wonder what a bottle of wine can do to strengthen the courage of a person, and can well imagine your satisfaction when you confront Steven with additional facts about all his lies, even though he is in a weak state. I'm amazed he continues to deny his behaviour, even though everything is now out in the open. I guess he's still trying to look favourable in your eyes. All I know is that he will never be trusted by me again, as when I blindly put ALL my trust in him in the past.

I'm astounded at the bits of information you are giving me about Steven's beguiling ways (at this stage I shouldn't really be surprised, but I am!!) That he was able to do "away" with your wedding rings, and probably pocketing the motel money that people paid him in cash. I now tend to think as you do, and agree that is probably how he managed it.

The older ring I mentioned in my earlier e-mail, that Steven said was his mother's wedding ring, does not sound like part of the set of your wedding bands, because they appear to be set with mother-of-pearl stones, and both stones are there, nothing is missing, unless he had them re-set, but you will see it for yourself when I send the rings back to you.

Thank you for letting me know what steps are being taken by the doctors concerning Steven's health. I'm sure though that not much can be done, if he's suffering and in so much pain, and unable to eat as he should. G-d, it's amazing, but I STILL feel sorry for him... ironic isn't it?

Do you read him the e-mails I've sent you? I know he has a lap top... does he have access to it while in hospital? On the other hand, I suppose he is too drugged by the pain killers that he probably just sleeps it off all day. Did you mention to him that I would still want one last contact with him, and if so, do you think he will try to reach me if he is at all able to once he gets home?

I'd appreciate it if you could let me know.

Donna, I wish you everything of the best and hope you too will look after yourself, G-d knows you will need all the strength you can get.

Best wishes,
Matty

From: Donna Lehl
Sent: Sunday, August 01, 2004 10:43 AM
To: 'Matty '
Subject: RE: Steven De Vore

Good Morning Matty – or Good Afternoon in Israeli time,

No, I don't read your letters to Steven. Even if he was well, he wouldn't be able to lip read anyone that long. That's why he is so much better at talking than letting someone else talk. I also have not given them to him to read because of his grogginess from medication. I only mention as much from your letters as I think shows his greatest callousness whenever he professes his undying love for me. It may help you get over him to know that he now refers to you as "the bitch" as though you did something to cause this situation. Count your blessings that you did not marry him and incur some legal responsibility for him and his expenses as I did. Be glad that you did not get to know the mean and hateful Steven. I encountered that side of him after we got married and many times I wished I had stayed single.

I also did not tell him that we were conspiring to have a meeting. I think that would be too much for him to contemplate at this time. I did not tell him that you had changed your initial decision to never have any contact with him. I will tell him that you would like him to contact you when he is able. He may be getting out of the hospital this week. Until then, his laptop is here because while he could use the laptop in certain areas of the hospital, he would not have Internet access, which is the only thing he cares about.

Please do not send back that ring of Steven's mother, unless you want me to give it back to him. I do recall he had such a ring and it does not sound like mine. I'll look in my jewelry box when I get back home; my rings are probably still there.

Take care,
Donna

Although I longed for a day off, I went to the hospital. I'm not sure if I went because I still loved him or, was it guilt or fear of appearing uncompassionate? It really didn't matter because there was no question that I would go and spend at least several hours with Steve in his room on the oncology ward. I wondered if he would have a roommate today. The man who had shared a room with him for the last ten days had "crashed" and Steve was abruptly moved, first to the hallway, then across the hall into an empty room, and then later around the corner, a trip from the nephrology ward to oncology. When I left him last night, he had been alone.

As soon as I rounded the corner from the elevator bank, I spotted him. He was walking down the hall, pushing his IV stand, assisted by the jovial Latina nurse, Luisa. When he saw me, he picked up speed and Luisa, apparently fearing a fall, reined him in by grasping the back of his gown. He was looking so much better. It was shocking, the difference a day could make.

"Hello, honey. I thought you would never get here," he said animatedly.

"I have missed you so much." I mumbled my now habitual refrain —"yeah, right," hoping Luisa would not hear me. I let him kiss my cheek and took over the walking assistance from the nurse.

We walked to the visitation room and back to his room while he chatted incessantly. He sure appeared to be feeling better and was just like his old self. He acted like nothing had changed between us when, in reality, everything had changed.

In a week's time, I had learned that I was the victim of infidelity and that I was soon to be a widow. Nothing would ever be the same again, ever. But I could see, up close and personal, the existence of one of the Unity principles — every problem comes with its own solution. I was married to a liar, a cheater, a thief, and a con artist. Soon enough he would be gone forever. I felt a little ashamed of these thoughts, as though I was wishing his demise. I really was not, but it clearly would be easier to forgive him if I didn't have to keep on living with him. I walked him back to his hospital bed and made a conscious effort to focus more on his needs.

When he got back to his bed, what he needed was another shot of morphine and a nap. The nurse provided the shot and the nap came automatically. I read the Sunday paper that I had brought from home and chatted with the wife of Steve's new roommate, a man named John who had some form of cancer that required him to be hospitalized for three to four days once a month for a continuous drip of chemotherapy. His wife, a very pleasant and well-spoken woman who worked for the school district, explained that this form of chemo made her husband very agitated and abusive as it built up in his system. Today was good. Tomorrow likely would not be good and the last day would be hell. Great, I can hardly wait until Tuesday, I thought sarcastically.

When Steve woke up, the nurse took his vitals, gave him his medications and told me that he was doing so well I could take him for a wheelchair ride around the hospital and even outside in the courtyard, if he wanted to go.

I found a wheelchair, got him up and into it, made sure he was decent, and gave him the IV stand to hold. I steered him down the hall, into the patient elevator and pushed the DOWN button. He acted genuinely excited to be leaving the seventh floor for something other than a test or surgery. It was the first time since his arrival. When we got to the first floor, I cruised by the flower and gift shop and down to the cafeteria, where Steve wanted to look at every food display. He finally settled on some macaroni and cheese, a piece of apple pie, and a cup of coffee. I parked him at a table and went back for our food.

"Here you go, your mac and cheese, a little cream in your coffee, napkin, and a fork. Do you need anything else?" I asked.

He shook his head and began nibbling little bits of his meal. We sat together in silence while I started eating my salad.

"I'm worried about the biopsy," he said. "They say I have to be awake, but you know how I panic. I can't be awake." He squeezed my hand and looked at me as if they were already about to insert the needle. "You have to tell them they need to put me out."

"You will be there, won't you honey?"

"I'll be there. I'll do what I can," I said halfheartedly, not because I didn't want to help him, but because I doubted my input would make a difference.

He always jokingly called me his mouthpiece — a slang term for lawyer. But I really had become his mouthpiece.

Because of his deafness and the accompanying speech impediment, I often needed to talk to others for him so that they could understand. Someone would ask him a question; he would look at me and read my lips as I repeated the question. Then he would answer. The questioner would look puzzled by what she heard, so I would then repeat what he had said. It was sort of a strange translation service where everyone was speaking the same language but only the translator could understand the dialects of the others. And now I knew I would again have to be his interpreter, since no one in hospitals takes the ADA (Americans with Disabilities Act) seriously, at least not if there's a family member available to help.

"Of course I'll be there with you." I reassured him again, my helping nature kicking in as I thought about my role as an advocate.

He pushed his half-full plate away and finished the coffee. "Let's get out of here."

The courtyard door was just outside of the cafeteria. We passed through the automatic doors out into the warm sunshine. Even though it was in the lower 80s, he shivered, so I wrapped the blanket I had thought to bring from his room over his shoulders. I pushed him around the little courtyard where there were ponds and fountains and children and birds, and where life looked oh so much better than inside on the nephrology/oncology ward, where people "crashing" was the norm. We sat for some time and watched a young family with two toddlers who kept climbing on the woman in a wheelchair. I wondered about her story and hoped it was nothing terminal that would take her away from them permanently. After three trips around the courtyard and then sitting for a while, I tried to interest him in the return trip. I had promised the nurses I would have him back in an hour.

"I don't want to go back there," he said. "Why don't you just take me home? I'll be good," he said, trying to be charming.

"You can't come home until they figure out what's wrong and how to fix it." I told him looking right at him so he could read my lips and know that I was serious. I wondered if they'd come looking for him or send security if we were gone longer than an hour. But mostly, I was just ready to take him back and head across town to my little apartment sanctuary. I needed a little break, since I doubted that I would be getting any rest anytime soon.

I got him back to his room in time for evening medication rounds and he dozed off within minutes of his morphine shot. I was free to go home and recharge my own batteries.

For once, there was nothing from Matty. Tomorrow I needed to be back at the hospital at 7:00 a.m. for the biopsy. I went to bed and slept as soon as I finished thinking: Lord, give me strength to endure my life.

The next day, the doctor who had been scheduled to perform the biopsy refused to do it. He met with us and began explaining what to expect during the procedure. Steve had to be awake so that he could hold his breath on command when the needle was inserted. He needed to be perfectly still so the needle would go to the right place. I could not be in the room during the procedure. Just how did he propose to communicate with a deaf man? I asked. I also told the doctor that Steve was prone to panic attacks and wanted to be placed under general anesthesia. I explained that Steve didn't think he could be still if he knew he was about to be stabbed with a very large needle. That was all it took for this wimpy, whiney resident to decide (probably because of malpractice issues) that he would not conduct the test on this patient.

"I won't do it, you can't make me," the doctor said as he stormed out of the preparation area. I had never seen a more unprofessional doctor and I was a bit relieved when he left.

By now, Steve was pretty worked up and had to urinate, but they told him to wait for a nurse to get him a urinal. Steve replied that he didn't need a urinal; he would walk to the restroom. When the nurse told him that he couldn't do that he responded with two words: "watch me," he said. I was left alone to handle him while the nurse ran off to get help. Knowing he would not be reasoned with, I walked him to the bathroom and held him and the IV as he relieved himself. When the nurse returned with a urinal and a male nurse, he was back on the gurney ready to go back to his room.

He complained and sputtered for an hour after he was transported back to his room. He and I rarely agreed on anything, but this was the exception – that spineless surgeon was lacking in both bedside manner and guts. But our sudden camaraderie didn't mean we had any idea what to do next.

I decided to go to work and come back later to talk to Doctor Newman or one of his associates. Perhaps they would have an idea how to complete the test they needed or to get the information in some other way.

"I'm going to work for a while, Steve," I said. "See if you can stay out of trouble for a few hours."

"Okay" he said, hanging his head. "I'm sorry, Honey. I just didn't like that guy and I figured he'd kill me with that needle."

"I know. You couldn't help yourself," I said, forcing my voice to be quiet while I was churning within and thinking – damn it, why couldn't you act like a grown-up for once.

I extricated my hand from his grasp and slipped out of the room before I lost control of myself and told him what I really thought. It wouldn't help the situation to unload on him. I knew he really was afraid.

When I came back that evening, I found Steve's neighbor beginning to rev up a barrage of profanities and verbal abuse that he directed toward his patient wife and dutiful daughter.

"Let's go for another ride." I loaded Steve into his wheelchair and headed for the elevator bank.

We had a nice visit. It was sort of like the good old days, except for the wheelchair, the IV pole, and the knowledge that it all would be coming to an end soon. We laughed and talked and pretended that life was good. And it was good on some level. We talked about the funny stuff the dogs had done and how much we looked forward to visiting my son Jeremy in Maui. Steve was optimistic that he would feel better soon and that he'd be able to make the trip in December. He held my hand and smiled at me like he used to do. For now we had each other, we had some nice memories and I was beginning to forgive him, or at least I was feeling compassion for him that took the edge off the feeling of betrayal.

When I finally got home that night and had completed the evening doggie-walk, feeding ritual, I was anxious to check the computer for the next installment from "the other woman."

From: Matty
Sent: Monday, August 02, 2004 2:38 AM
To: Donna
Subject: Steven De Vore

Hello Donna, Good Morning to you,

I am truly thankful that I did not get to the point of eventually marrying Steven (G-d knows he often urged me to do so...often calling me his wife) and as you say, incurring further expenses for his up-keep. Even if all this did not come out in the open, I wouldn't have known how to handle or to cope with his illness (the cancer). It would hurt me too much to see him dying little by little each day, especially after all the plans we had made for our future lives together.

So now I am "the bitch" in this entire

situation - what a laugh that is! Amazing how he could transfer all his "loving feelings" for me so easily back to you. He probably has a hatred for me for ruining all his plans. I guess he has to show his undying love for you, because he now knows that his life is short, and he is still dependant on you to help and support him, and if he was left destitute by you he no longer has the time nor the strength to entice some other poor innocent victim into his web of lies and deceit. Then where would he be?

I've been curious to know how you two met and how he treated you whilst you were dating and after you got married. When did the true face of Steven show itself to you and what gave you the strength to remain in this marriage? Did you ever try to investigate or make contact with his previous ex-wives to learn why he had been divorced so many times? (Despite the reasons he told you, which could also have been lies).

I hope you don't think I'm prying into your private life by asking you all these questions, but I'm trying to figure out what makes Steven tick. To me it appears he may have a split personality - at one time showing his warm, caring and loving side and then attaining whatever he was after - showing his mean and hateful side. To me he also professed his undying love, and said he would give his life up for me and protect me at any cost if anything should happen to me. He was so charming and convincing and played the role of a lover very well and claiming to be loyal only to me. What a farce it all was!

I have a feeling that since he became deaf at the age of 7, which he told me was from some under-water explosion, and being raped in the orphanage by the nuns and priests there, that he went into some kind of fantasy world, and to protect himself from there on, a seed of revenge, and a struggle to survive in this world, made him want to ensure that he could get women to feel some kind of pity for him and to take care of his needs. He convinced himself of the lies he was telling and acted it out very well. I am no psychoanalyst, but that's just my opinion as I see it.

Another one of his stories he told me, was that while serving in the Middle East he had met up with an Israeli woman soldier. A romance developed between them. After a while she became pregnant with his child, but later died during one of the wars. He was so enraged and remorseful that afterwards he decided to go through with the process of becoming sterile. Ironic how I fell for all these sob stories.

I've often wondered if he really cared or asked how I was doing and how I was taking it all when his deceit came out in the open - he knows what a sensitive and emotional person I am... before he started calling me "the bitch" that is - I am laughing cynically here at the turn of circumstances. Guess we both won't know what really was behind it all.

Anyway Donna, there are so many more stories I could tell you about Steven and the life he told me he led, but that I will leave at a later stage if you are interested in knowing.

I'm happy that you haven't told him that we may be planning to meet. We'll see how things work out as time goes by.

Take care and best wishes,
Matty

My reply nearly wrote itself:

From: Donna Lehl
Sent: Monday, August 02, 2004 11:55 PM
To: 'Matty '
Subject: Steven De Vore

My dear friend Matty,

I never thought I'd ever feel such affection for the "other woman," but somehow it's different because I am certain you were not trying to break up another woman's home. While reading your letter, I had a brilliant idea – I will write a book. I now have a story worth telling and reading. This is a peek at my character and maybe a bit of understanding for you why I stayed. I have learned over the years to make lemonade of the lemons in my life.

I stayed when things became strained because I understand, intellectually at least, that when someone is not happy with themselves, they often find it easier to strike out at those around them than to face the reality that we each have responsibility for making ourselves happy. I also stayed because I have been divorced once before after an 18-year marriage and I knew that a change of scenery, a change of partners, didn't bring happiness. In retrospect, I wish I had been mature enough in my first marriage to keep working on it. And I stayed for the reason you mentioned – Steve could be so sweet, apologetic, charming, convincing. He caused me to forgive him over and over again. I am still able to forgive him. I just can't ever trust him again.

We met through a dating service – one that charged quite a bit of money for the express purpose of weeding out the "losers." It was supposed to be "safe" because they claimed to do criminal background checks, etc. We entered a romantic and physical relationship quite quickly after our first date. I was particularly attracted to his sensitivity when he described a friend of his who had some chronic health condition for whom Steven championed for work place changes. He was very affectionate toward me for the first three years or so of our relationship – told me he loved me several times a day, constantly hugging and kissing me. He asked me to marry him when we had only been together a short while – a month or so. I didn't want to commit so soon because I had been disappointed in love once or twice. It actually took me three years to say okay, let's get married, and then it was sort of a function of two things – he was here to stay anyway and I probably couldn't do much better (a little low self-esteem in action) and he had convinced me that our sex life was suffering because he felt so insecure. He knew I could just tell him to leave whenever I wanted and he would have no rights because the house, the business and everything we had was mine except for his pickup truck, his dog and his computer.

Steve showed his really negative traits over time. He was very critical of many people, filled with hate for and prejudice against many groups. That bothered me, but I have had no success in trying to get him to be more charitable. He totally alienated my father, my sister, my sister-in-law, two good friends of mine, and most people I know would just rather not be around him. He was rude to me in their presence, openly hostile toward some of them, and he often talked dirty in mixed company when such conduct was not appropriate. I'm no prude, but I know when to avoid rough language. He became my constant critic to the point that I either ignored him or lashed out at him. Sometimes it wasn't very pretty. But honestly I can't say he ever revealed his true self to me because I never would have guessed the revelations of the past week.

Reading about his explanation to you of his deafness made me laugh and shake my head, but then I realized he's probably told me some whoppers too, like going to a pasta sauce competition in Italy and winning a medal which one of his wives stole from him. He also told me he had been sexually abused as a child, which he used (along with his diabetes) to explain his lack of sexual interest.

Matty, I regret to tell you that he has shown absolutely no remorse for what he did to you even though I told him he had devastated you and caused you great pain and I told him that he ought to make amends to you for his deceit. He continues to try to convince me that all he wants is to regain my trust and to get back the life we had before we "fought all the time." He does not have enough contact with reality to know those days are gone forever.

I agree that Steve probably has some sort of mental health issue, but as an undergraduate psychology major (meaning I know just enough to make me dangerous), I would say it is more likely that he is a sociopath – the lying, the manipulation, the lack of true concern for others. But there are also indications he may be manic-depressive (bipolar). He has periods of lethargy, depression, little activity followed by very expansive fantasy-like thinking and acting out. He probably does believe some of his own lies. At any rate, I believe his deafness, his childhood, and possibly other experiences in his life have all contributed to his mental state. That's no excuse, but it does shed some light.

Here's his health report. He will have a liver biopsy whenever they schedule it (again). If the spots on his liver are cancerous, they will not offer radiation. He has perked up the last two days and is beginning to eat a little. Tonight I took him by wheel-chair down to the cafeteria. It was a real outing to him after two weeks in a hospital room. He is still taking a lot of pain medication and acted shocked and depressed when I told him what he was taking was quite addictive. I don't know what he thought he was taking (some super-strong aspirin?)

Well Matty, it's time for me to get ready for bed. I feel like when we get tired of talking about him, we'll be over him. Perhaps I'm a little further along that path than you because for a long time I have been with him out of a feeling of responsibility and a belief that when God is satisfied that I have learned all that I need from my relationship with Steve that he will move on out of my life. I hope you find some positive reason for this experience and we are both able to move beyond the pain soon.

Best Wishes,
Donna

From: Matty
Sent: Tuesday, August 03, 2004 11:04 AM
To: Donna
Subject: Parcel on the way

Dear Donna,

Just a short e-mail to let you know that today I have sent you the parcel containing the rings, pendant and other bits and pieces. I just hope that it reaches you safely.

I'm not sure that the box is small enough to fit through your mail box, so you may be getting a notice from your local post office that a package is awaiting you. It should take about 3 to 5 days to get to you. Please let me know once you've received it, as some of the contents are very precious.

I will answer your last e-mail to me either later this evening, or sometime tomorrow.

Yours sincerely,
Matty

From: Matty
Sent: Tuesday, August 03, 2004 2:45 PM
To: Donna
Subject: Steven De Vore

Dearest Donna.

Thank you for calling me your friend, and showing your affection for "the other woman." I feel honoured in a way, and it does seem strange this bond that has been forged between us. I too feel a closeness to you, and I guess it's because we have kept up a constant communication between the two of us and our openness in our common situation. It was never my intention to break up your home. Lord knows I shy away from such occurrences, and Steven also knew that if I had any inkling of his married status, that I would have broken off the relationship.

I also thank you for taking the time to answer all my questions and giving me some idea of the life you have led whilst being married to Steven and when you were dating him. I know you are probably kept very busy with all your work, and also visiting Steven every evening and seeing to his needs. It must be so exhausting for you rushing around everywhere and therefore your timely e-mail replies are very much appreciated by me.

I had to chuckle when you wrote that you had a brilliant idea about writing a book, because I have a very close friend who knew about my relationship with Steven since we started chatting, and she suggested I do exactly the same thing - tell my story and to have it printed in a magazine - but I doubt I'll do such a thing.

It hurt me to read about Steven's treatment of you and how he alienated you from your family and friends, and criticized you in front of them. I think that was really despicable of him and don't blame you for ignoring him or lashing out at him sometimes because I'm sure it was most embarrassing for you.

I met Steven in a chat room 2 ½ years ago and though I was very wary about having a one-on-one chat with him, he eventually convinced me there wouldn't be any harm to it - just an innocent chat between friends. We had a mutual friend on the chat whom he knew long before me, and when I asked her if she thought it would be safe to chat with him she said, "I would trust him with my life" which encouraged me to go ahead and get to know him as a friend. One often hears about all the pitfalls about how dangerous it can get when meeting people on the chat, and yet sometimes there are also success stories. Anyway, I thought it might be pleasant to get to know Steven and chat with him as a friend (something like a pen-pal). I had no intention at all of getting romantically involved with him. He was actually afraid to tell me in the beginning about his deafness, because he thought I might have snubbed him, but when he did eventually tell me after we had been communicating for about 3 weeks, I told him it made no difference to me. I considered him first and foremost as a person with feelings and emotions and not someone with an impairment to be ignored. This statement I think gave him the courage to turn this innocent chat we had between us into more romantic terms. According to Steven, he later told me it was very hard for him to get me romantically involved with him because I didn't want to commit to anything at that stage. I was too afraid.

We would not chat every day - maybe once or twice a week or whenever it worked out for him to come on-line, because he would tell me that he would be sent out on "missions" from time to time by the military - fighting in Afghanistan and Iraq and various places in the Middle East. He said he would be "retiring from the military" during that first year, and even after his retirement we would not chat that often since he was being sent to some "rehabilitation centre" to be able to learn to adjust to civilian life, since all his needs had been taken care of by the military (food, clothing, housing etc.) and now he had to learn to fend for himself in the everyday world.

After being in rehab, he was moved to "Dee's" home, where she supposedly kept an eye on his progress (she too was a lawyer, but also worked for the military in the capacity for looking after such military men) and received his pension cheques for his up-keep. Soon after, he was more free to keep up with daily chats between us.

Steven was very loving and caring towards me also saying that he loved me after every few sentences, which boosted my ego, since I too had been divorced for 15 years and also had a few disappointments with love. I could not believe that a person could show me so much attention, encouragement, warmth and love, and made me feel desired. My self-confidence was so very low and Steven managed to strengthen my belief in me as a person. That at least is a positive thing about his charm.

I've no need to tell you Donna, that on the two occasions he came to Israel, his attitude towards me was exactly the same as when on the chat and even more so. Like when he was dating you. He would never stop hugging and kissing me, holding me close, telling me every now and then that he loves me and giving me so much attention. We hardly stayed apart from one another and our lovemaking was so beautiful and tender, an idyllic honeymoon romance.

Yes, when my friends also came to dine he also talked dirty, but it was done in a fun way. I laughed but also felt embarrassed at the same time, but he would take me and hug me and showed me so much affection. We did everything together - housework, chores, preparing meals, preparing for our trips together, fixing things around the apartment. It was all so harmonious and compatible.

It's too bad he doesn't show any remorse for the pain and devastation he caused me, but I suppose that's to be expected. Obviously now he has to show his favourable side to you in order for you to forgive him. I just hope for your sake he's not faking it, and this time he will be true to his words, though it's understandable that it will be difficult for you to trust him again. As for me, only time will heal all the wounds.

Anyway, I'm happy to hear that Steven has perked up a bit, and I'm sure that outing to the cafeteria was a pleasant change for him after staying two weeks in a hospital room. I'm sure it must have lifted his morale to see a change in scenery. Please tell him from me that despite the hardships I'm going through right now, I'm compassionate enough to wish him well and hopefully, if one can say it, a speedy recovery.

I don't know if I've read you right, between the lines, but if you feel you want to stop writing to me about Steven, please say so. I'll understand. I would only want to know from you any updates about his health situation please, or if I can ask you any further questions from time to time that might suddenly occur to me, if that would be alright?

Take care my dear Donna. All the very best to you.

Matty

I reread the section of Matty's letter where she discussed Steve's military career and his subsequent rehabilitation. I laughed long and loud when imagining Steve on missions in Iraq and Afghanistan. The dogs looked at me quizzically. I couldn't help thinking that Matty was extremely naive and some part of me felt a little bit superior for not being *that* stupid. And the crazy story about Dee — a lawyer whose job it was to look after soldiers and sort of act as their guardian was a real hoot! Steve obviously had an overactive imagination and a way of dragging others into it.

As much as I wanted to address the many things in Matty's message, the day had left me spent. Trying to work full time, visit Steve and manage his affairs at night, and taking care of the dogs and the apartment was beginning to take its toll. Tonight I drove halfway home in the dark without any headlights and absent-mindedly missed my exit so that I ended up traveling six miles out of my way. I decided to forego the long response and the scotch and soda that was usually required to produce a long and thoughtful reply. I would just write a few words in case Matty looked forward to hearing from me as much as I did hearing from her.

From: Donna Lehl
Sent: Tuesday, August 03, 2004 11:26 PM
To: 'Matty '
Subject: RE: Steven De Vore

Matty,

I want to continue our conversation. I think it is therapeutic for both of us and your stories give me more material for the book I would like to write someday. However, as you guessed, I am exhausted. Tonight I am like a zombie. I barely made it home from the hospital and couldn't stay awake during a little mindless TV. I'll reply as soon as I feel a little more rested.

Until then, my friend,
Donna

Chapter Four

The New Normal

Two days passed before I felt able to write again and I was anxious to pick up the story where we left off.

From: Donna Lehl
Sent: Thursday, August 05, 2004 11:48 PM
To: 'Matty '
Subject: Steven De Vore

Hi Matty,

I have been so tired the last few days that I've been walking around like a Zombie and last night I had the added stress (albeit pleasant stress) of meeting with a man who may be interested in buying my motel. It would be so wonderful if I could get rid of it and have one less thing to worry about. It's not doing me any good now with no one to run it during the peak of the season. Anyway, he's not talking about the kind of deal I'd like to have, but it is still better than having all of that extra expense and no benefit.

My friends, family and coworkers have all been so supportive of me, calling all the time, taking me out to lunch or dinner, and just stopping by my office to chat. A very few of them know of the added twist — that I learned about you because of Steve's illness and hospitalization.

I've done a lot of reviewing now of all those instances in which I thought what he told me was either too fantastic to believe or "fishy" in some way. He was probably lying each and every time and probably many other times when I didn't have a clue. He went to California to visit some newly found relatives of his dad about three years ago. The months leading up to that trip started our alienation. For a period of time he would do nothing all day except chat on the Internet, while I worked. And he made arrangements to go visit these "relatives." I didn't think too much about it because I knew he had some relatives there that he had just discovered because an aunt, cousin and her husband came to visit us. But, when he decided to go see them, he made it clear I wasn't welcome to come along even though my son lived in another part of California and I really wanted to go. I know now that he was probably using these relatives as a cover for his true purpose — to visit some other woman he met online.

I now feel like his "conversion" had some hidden element as well. He was careful to keep me from any contact with anyone from the Shul. He asked me for cash for various contributions saying that Jews don't take checks for such purposes. He either planned to use the money for something else, or he wanted to make sure that the Rabbi did not see my name on his checks. What is also funny is that I e-mailed his Rabbi to let her know of his illness and hospitalization and I have heard nothing since and I don't think he has heard from anyone in the congregation either. During his attendance there, he claimed that his Rabbi had a fiancé and that they got married shortly after his return from the first trip to see you. He brought them a candelabra as a wedding gift. Without confirmation of his story from someone else, I suspect he may have been trying to make a move on the Rabbi as well.

How horrible it is to have to have regular contact with and be responsible for someone you cannot believe at all. I don't feel that I will ever feel differently no matter how hard he tries to convince me of his sincerity. In your last message you say you hope for my sake that he is not "faking it." I can't believe that he is doing anything else but faking it. And I guess I'm faking it too because I do not share my really angry feelings with him.

I am sending you a few pictures so you will get a small view of the horrible life he had with me. The first is a recent picture of Steve and his dog walking along the river on our property. This was taken just a couple of months ago (after his return from you) when he was already quite ill. The next one was Steve on the beach during our vacation last December-January. He probably told you some wild story about what he was doing then so that he couldn't contact you. And the last one is the one that hurts me most – it is the picture of Steve at the airport on his way to meet you in person the first time. Of course, I had no idea and I brought him there, saw to it he got through security and was ready to get on the plane. Had I known what he was doing, I probably would not have picked him up there three weeks later.

Oh, I got a message from the post office that they need my signature on a package from Israel, so apparently your package has already arrived.

It's late Matty, so I better get into bed so I can do it all over again tomorrow. Steve may be getting out of the hospital within the next couple of days. I'll let you know what happens.

Warm regards,
Donna

From: Matty
Sent: Saturday, August 07, 2004 2:20 AM
To: Donna
Subject: Steven De Vore

Good Morning Donna,

I do hope you slept a little bit better last night. I can imagine all the exhaustion you must be going through with everything on your head - your work, taking care of Steven and thinking about running your motel. I'm sure thinking about this situation that's cropped up between all of us has left you mentally exhausted too. Believe me, there are many nights I don't sleep as well and find myself waking up in the very early hours of the morning, unable to stop thinking of all that's been till now. How I manage to concentrate at work G-d only knows.

I do hope you succeed in selling your motel off, even though the deal is not what you would liked to have had. At least it will be one less headache for you, and as you say, would be difficult without anyone to run it for you now. Is your motel in Tawas City and do you also own a marina?

I am happy to know that your friends and coworkers are supporting you in this distressful time. It warms the heart to know that people care and are concerned, and hopefully what you share with your close friends helps to slightly lift the burden that you must be feeling in your heart.

Steven also told me that about three years ago he had discovered some family from his father's side living in California. I understood from Steven that he was from Canadian/American Indian descent. His father was Canadian, had four sisters - three of whom Steven had never met since they had died in the meantime, and the one remaining aunt living in California who died recently, just a few months ago, and that he also had a few cousins. Steven's mother was American Indian (Cherokee) who died while giving birth to him. His grandmother from his mother's side took care of him, till she herself became too ill to see to his needs, and the authorities put him in an orphanage. According to Steven, his father was also in the military fighting in the Middle East. After his first wife died, his father remarried and that he had two step-sisters and a step-brother, whom Steven found out about much later in life, but as he did not get on with them, decided to cut off all ties.

When his father returned home from one of his missions and found out that Steven had been placed in an orphanage, he had him removed from there, and put in military school till the age of 17, where afterwards he was enlisted in the army and fought in Vietnam, then trained to be an agent and was sent on missions all over the world.

I cried at the stories that Steven would tell me about his childhood - how he had been sexually abused, the hardships he faced about being deaf and how many times he had to fight and struggle from the beatings and being taunted by all around him. Is this all true? I don't know what he told you of his background and younger days, but like you, I tend to believe he was in an orphanage and probably abused also. As for the rest, one can only speculate. The thing is that I've seen many scars on his arms and body which he claimed were bullet wounds (although he was protected with a bullet-proof vest), knife and sword wounds.

The only thing that I know of his conversion was that he was taking classes and attending shul (temple) services maybe once a month on Friday nights. He told me he had made friends with an old couple there, and that in time the congregation there gave him a warm welcome. I would help him with his homework and the discussions between us were always so interesting.

Yes, when he did come here the first time he did buy a candelabra for his Rabbi when she got married, but if he made any moves on her, I was not aware of it. The cash he took from you I believe was given for various contributions since he sent me a certificate of acknowledgement mentioning people that had donated various sums and Steven's name was included on the list besides sending me one or two receipts of other donations he had given. It does seem strange though that his Rabbi did not e-mail you when you told her of his illness.

As for your holiday you took last December-January, you guessed it, another lie from Steven. He told me his cousin in California was involved in a very bad car accident, and that he had to go out there to take care of her and to relieve the rest of his family till they could organise to have a nurse come in to look after her - and now too I'm discovering through you that he also had another woman he met on-line? My G-d, where does it all end?

You said in your e-mail that you are "faking it" because you do not share your angry feelings with him.... does this mean he is unaware that we are e-mailing each other and telling our sides of the story? If that is the case, I'm sure he would cringe to know that he's been found out regarding his lies and deceit, if he had any conscience at all.

I would like to receive the photos you wanted to send - maybe you can send them separately at another time, when you are able. I'm only sorry for the heartache you go through when you see those pictures... I too have pictures of Steven and I which hurt me when I look at them, and remember how fantastic it was between us, which can now no longer be.

Oh, I just received your e-mail about

receiving the parcel. I'm happy to know that it arrived safely and you have your amethyst ring back... I too cannot imagine how Steven could give me something so precious belonging to his wife and claim it to be my engagement ring... it is a beautiful ring and I too treasured it, because it made our relationship that much firmer and closer.

I thank you for your offer of sending a piece of your jewellery, but I cannot accept - I'd feel too embarrassed and don't want you going into any extra expense on my behalf, but it is a lovely thought which is much appreciated. I do pray for peace in the world and most especially for inner peace for the both of us.

Donna, I wish you all the strength and calm that you can find.

Warm regards to you.
Matty

From: Donna Lehl
Sent: Saturday, August 07, 2004 10:30 PM
To: 'Matty '
Subject: Steven De Vore

Hi Matty,

Thank you for your kind wishes. I slept well last night (actually for the past week I've been sleeping like a dead person because I'm so darn tired all the time). And, I had the most glorious three hours this morning. I went to a salon and had a pedicure, complete with foot massage and pretty polish on the nails; then

I had my hair cut, colored and highlighted. I spent nearly $200, never done that before, but it was worth every penny to rest, relax and have people pamper me. I doubt that I will make a habit of anything but the pedicure (I need a hip replacement and cannot twist my left foot into position to cut my own toe nails), but it was a lovely indulgence.

I heard that the showing of my motel went well, that they were talking about what they would do when they are there. I hope that it will soon be just a memory of one of my adventures (or misadventures).

As for Steven's heritage, I doubt that he knows for sure. He apparently has some Indian blood (he looks it and his grandmother on his father's side appears very Native American from pictures I have seen). When we met, he told me he was Sioux (a tribe present in the Dakotas). He referred to them as "his people" and we went to powwows (Native Gatherings) and he spent quite a bit of money on collectibles with a Sioux connection and he bought a necklace made of bone, I think, that he wore when we got married with his suit instead of a tie. When he found his father's family, they told him he was part Cherokee (a tribe present in the south part of this country). His name is French which I'm sure is part of the reason he adopted the "French Canadian" heritage, which may also have come from my mother's family who can trace their roots to the Montreal area – another French name.

Steve's mother did not die giving birth to him unless he has convinced some poor old woman in California that he is her son. I met her about four or five years ago and she was quite a pleasant woman. This was before Steve found his father's family and he had made amends with his mother for giving him to a nun at age two, who took him to an orphanage to be raised (all according to the story Steve told me of his early years). One thing I noticed during that visit was that he absolutely hated for Kathryn and I to spend any time talking alone. I thought it was because he doesn't share well, but now I think he was afraid we would "compare notes" and "blow his cover," revealing all his lies to one or the other (or both) of us. During that visit with his mother, he convinced me to buy her a TV/VCR set so she would have a decent set to play the videos on that he would send her. Within a year he had found some relatives of his father and he cut all ties with her. One of the last letters he received from her, he let me read and it made reference to things that one of his ex-wives had written to her about him. He used those comments as examples of her meddling and justification for cutting off contact with her. I have had some minimal contact with her since then, but not for the last year or so. Now when I ask Steve if he'd like me to tell his mother of his illness he says "my mother is dead."

You asked me once in one of your letters whether I ever tried to contact any of Steve's ex-wives. No, never, but I may consider it now since I know he is a pathological liar and I definitely will try to contact his mother for more information about his life and his wives.

The only thing I heard her say about Steve's childhood when I met her is that he spent a lot of it at school (which I took to mean California School for the Deaf).

Maybe the stories about the conversion are true and maybe his Rabbi did actually get married, but there is something there and I don't know what it is. I think they don't know that he was married to me. That is probably why his wedding ring (very expensive, special design he demanded) suddenly became too large so that he couldn't wear it. I have since bought him a plain gold band that he wore until he had a procedure that couldn't be done with jewelry and I brought it home. She still has not responded to my e-mail nor has she or any member of the congregation visited him. Isn't that strange?

Don't feel bad about his war wounds any longer. I am fairly certain that he never fought in any war except for a long battle with his conscience. The scars you saw on his arms, he told me came from welding. This could also be a lie, but it makes more sense than bullet wounds, unless from one of the many women he has hurt.

No, Steve doesn't know that we have become "pen pals," but if I know him at all he will as soon as he gets out of the hospital and spends a day here while I am at work. He will be on my computer and reading everything. He may even try to delete all of our conversations, but I have saved everything in hard copy in a safe place. Steve is very concerned about his own privacy, probably so that he won't get caught, but he has no respect for the privacy of anyone else.

Didn't you think it strange that he would send you receipts for contributions that he made? I think that it is strange that he did not give them to me to reduce our taxes.

As for the photos, you should have received the one of Steve and his dog. Attached to this message will be the picture of Steve at the airport coming to you the first time. It's hard for me to believe that I helped him pack, drove him to the airport, and helped him get through security so that he could go off with another woman and cheat on me.

Finally, it is too late. I have put the little gift to you in the mail today. It is not expensive and as I said, I bought it for myself to remind me to pray for peace. It is now a habit, I don't have to remind myself any longer and I sincerely want you to have peace in your country and in your heart. Please keep it when it arrives.

Today Steve was really sleepy. I think they had just a little too much pain medication in him. I took him outside for a little while. We didn't talk much. We just both enjoyed the fresh air and flowers in the hospital garden and we probably each had our own pleasant (I hope) thoughts.

Good Night Matty,
Donna

From: Matty
Sent: Sunday, August 08, 2004 7:43 AM
To: Donna
Subject: Steven De Vore

My Dear Donna,

I was pleased to read that you went out and decided to spoil yourself by having your hair done and having a pedicure. Though it does sound rather expensive, I believe in spoiling one's self from time to time. It's not something you do every week, and believe me, you don't take money to the grave, so if you can pamper yourself every few months, go for it. Not only does it make you feel a different person, but it also makes one feel good about one's self. Funnily enough, I thought of doing the same thing myself, but have not really been in the mood for it. Many a time I told Steven that I felt like cutting my hair short (I have shoulder length hair) but he always told me not to, because then it would feel to him like he was kissing a man and that he liked women with fairly long hair and he liked to play with my hair and run his fingers through it when we were in bed, and burying his face around my neck and smelling me all over.

Steven told me that his surname was spelt at one time in the French style - De Veaux - but he said that since some people found it difficult to pronounce, he decided to change the spelling to De Vore. It now brings me to wonder if that too was a lie. Reading through your e-mail you mention that you actually met up with Steven's mother about four to five years ago, and that her name was Kathryn? The reason I am puzzled by this is that I have seen proof of his birth certificate (a copy of which I obtained from another source) and the mother's name mentioned there is Mary De Vore (note that the surname is "De Vore") unless as you say, he convinced some poor old woman that he is her son, but then according to what you say there seems to be conflicting statements, but it must have really been his mother. She may have decided to change her name from Mary to Kathryn. Despite the fact that Steven did not like you spending time alone with her, she was able to tell you that most of his childhood was spent at school. It would be interesting to know what his mother could tell you about Steven, if you were able to contact her and if she really is still alive. It may be a thought too, to contact the California School for the Deaf if anyone is still there to remember Steven's school days (which may be wishful thinking since so many years have gone by). Did Steven still keep contact with her after his separation from her in his youth and was able to find her once again?

I am still amazed at all this information we are finding out about Steven from each other, but I guess by now, I shouldn't be surprised. There seem to be "bits" of truth mixed in with so many lies and deceit - the whole thing just seems so bizarre. All I can say is that Steven was very cunning and clever to go through with it all, because one would have to have a very good memory to remember all the lies and what he said to whom.

As for the receipts I received from Steven regarding the contributions he gave, I don't know what to think. I guess he wanted to prove to me that he indeed did give various sums to charities and that I would be proud of him for doing so, and not just something he mentioned while we were chatting. I'm sure that neither his Rabbi nor the congregation were aware that he was married, since he mentioned that they were so happy he had found a girlfriend in Israel, but sad at the thought that he was going to be leaving them to come settle here. It does seem strange though that his Rabbi did not contact you about his illness. I really do wonder now whether he did go all the way with his conversion. Steven did show me the certificate he received after he converted through the web cam. It appeared real enough, but who knows if it wasn't forged? (In truth, I somehow believe it was for real).

I did notice a few weeks ago in one of our chats that all of a sudden Steven was wearing what looked to be a wedding band on his left finger which he had never worn before and when I asked him about it, he told me it belonged to his father. In a way I thought it was strange, since he had told me that his father died somewhere in the desert and his body was never found, so how could he get hold of his father's ring? I remember questioning him about it and he gave me some kind of convincing answer which I can't recall at this time, but still thought something was fishy, and just let it go at that.

Donna, I think you are very wise to have saved our e-mails to each other on a hard disk and kept in a safe place. I don't know how Steven would react if he find out. I am no computer expert, and in fact very illiterate where it comes to computers and their functions, but as I understand from you, Steven has access to your computer, meaning that he must know the passwords you use. You mentioned in one of your letters that he worked in "computer crime" which he also told me about. As far as I know, Steven was a real expert in computers and often helped me to set up the simplest of things which I found difficulty with and many times advising people on the chat about different programmes, etc. Now, as I mentioned to you before, Steven whilst here was working on and updating my computer. I know he installed for me an updated version of an anti-virus and a firewall and blocking certain sites on the Internet if I wanted to surf that had viruses and Trojans. He actually did a very good job, but if he is such a computer expert, I just hope he did not do anything to my computer that would allow him access to take it over or to enable him to plant viruses or crash it (just to get some sort of revenge on me). Maybe I'm being paranoid, but I don't know what to think any more.

Thank you for sending me the picture of Steven when he first came to Israel. He always looks so serious and I once asked him why he never smiled. He said he had nothing in his life to smile about which I replied I intended to change. All I wanted was for him to forget all the unhappiness he had in the past and to look forward to a better future with me by his side.

As for the picture of Steven and his dog - that I did not receive at all.

I hope Steven is feeling a little better,

though he is so drugged from all the medication. I'm sure once he gets home and out of the hospital environment it may make a difference to his morale and hopefully lift his spirits a bit. I'm sure it will be slightly easier on you too, not having to run to the hospital every evening.

Take care Donna.

Best wishes,
Matty

From: Matty
Sent: Sunday, August 08, 2004 9:46 AM
To: Donna
Subject: Steven De Vore

Dear Donna,

Just wanted to correct myself on the last e-mail I sent you... I took another look at Steven's birth certificate and one of the names appearing for his birth mother is Kathryn... her name is actually Mary Berta Kathryn.

I apologise for this oversight... now your e-mail makes more sense to me why you called her Kathryn.

Regards,
Matty

From: Matty
Sent: Monday, August 09, 2004 1:55 PM
To: Donna
Subject: Pictures
Dear Donna,

Thank you for sending the pictures. I have now received all 3 of them. The picture taken with you, Steven and your parents is lovely and they look like such a sweet couple.

Hope all is well with you.

Best regards,
Matty

From: Donna Lehl
Sent: Monday, August 09, 2004 10:44 PM
To: 'Matty '
Subject: RE: Steven De Vore

Hi Matty,

I just returned from the hospital. Yes, he is still in the hospital. Today after two particularly bad days, Steve perked up a little and started eating again, took an interest in his treatment and seemed to have his pain under better control. The doctors want to do a sort of "nerve block" for pain, actually killing some of the nerve cells that tell the brain something is wrong. He is thinking about it.

After receiving your last message, I have a favor to ask of you. Unless I ask about something specific, please don't tell me anymore about your intimate times together. I know they happened, but to be honest, it makes me sick to my stomach and terribly jealous. I have been lonely and depressed and horny for a very long time and somehow it was easier when I believed he was not capable of having a sexual relationship. Now I know he just didn't want me — quite a bruise to my sagging self-esteem. Anyway, I don't blame you. I'd just rather not know more of the details of that aspect of your relationship with him.

Steve's name has never been De Veaux. He has read about the origins of family groups and it is widely believed that the De Vore, De Voe, De Vos names all come from the French De Veaux or De Vereaux. I think this is how Steve thinks about his whole life. He is just a little bit disconnected from it. So anything he reads or sees on TV can become a part of his imaginings, day dreams or what have you. Then somewhere along the line he "tries out" the fantasy by telling it to someone and before long, it becomes a part of the history he tells himself and others.

He has many times told me about some strange thing that happened during the day. Honestly, I don't believe that much interesting happened during his days that he did not learn second-hand and somehow weave into his "story." I used to wonder why these things only happened when I wasn't there. Now I think I know.

You're right about the mixing of truth and fiction. It's impossible with Steve to tell where one leaves off and the other begins. And I believe you are also right about his being quite clever. He has good intelligence, but more than that he has "street smarts." He instinctively knows people, what they need, what will put them off, what will satisfy their curiosity when they begin to trust their own instincts. He knows how to play me —he knows I respond to guilt and a sense of fairness. So all he has to do to get me where he wants me is to make me feel guilty or like I am not being fair. I'm sure he knows your "buttons" too – probably your big heart and always making you feel sorry for him.

I also believe he completed his conversion, but how invested he is in the religion or in worshiping God, I don't know. I sort of think it was a means to an end for him. I'm not sure though what that end was – maybe being able to start over in Israel with you taking care of him instead of me. He probably hasn't yet figured out that the "grass is not really greener on the other side of the fence." And, wherever he goes, he needs to deal with his own issues, whatever they are.

The one thing Steve has probably not exaggerated is his ability to deal with computers. He probably is capable of hacking your computer, but somehow I don't think that he would do anything to make it inoperable. I would be more concerned about his ability to snoop. He knows about computers and programs from his previous work and from the many magazines to which he subscribes. I don't believe now that he really was an official fighting computer crime. He probably had a good imagination for such things and could figure out how hackers operated (maybe doing it himself) so that he was useful in figuring out how to prevent breaches.

He liked thinking of himself as "law enforcement" as he did calling himself "a chef," "a cowboy," "a legal assistant," "a computer guru," "a commercial fisherman," "a building contractor," "a soldier," "an Indian" "a Jew."

There is an American author by the name of James Thurber who wrote a short story (I think it was a short story) called The Secret Life of Walter Mitty. It has been maybe 35 years since I read it, but I remember the main character being like Steve. I am going to look for it when I get to a book store next. You might also find it amusing.

Here's another little tidbit you may find interesting. During the first seven or eight years or so of our relationship, Steve absolutely hated being called Steven. He would correct me if I ever slipped up and called him that. He wanted to be called only Steve. Then after getting involved with you, he became Steven, then eventually Z'ev, or however it is spelled. In between he thought of himself as "Wolfwalker" and would occasionally (usually after too much to drink) chant in the same way I have heard Native Americans do at their powwows. I always wondered how he knew to make the same sound, which he likely never heard.

Finally, regarding the question you asked about his contact with his mother. Yes, as I understood it, he had contact with her sporadically over the years. Sometimes when he was young he would run away from whatever school he was in (maybe the reformatory, for all I know) and he would go home to his mother. Then after he moved to Michigan, he would be angry with her and not talk to her for years; then he would decide to forgive her and resume contact. He was in somewhat regular contact with her throughout our time together until about three years ago when he found out about his father dying in about 1986. I think it was 1986. Steve had looked for information about him for years and (according to Steve) had been told by his mother for many years that he was dead. As far as I know, he has not had contact with her since, although I had some courteous contact with her on occasion until maybe a year and a half ago.

You know Matty, where Steve really fooled me was convincing me that he would always be loyal and affectionate to me. It is that belief that caused me to overlook the unhappiness, the sexual frustration, and the resentment that he did not pull his weight financially, and to settle for him as a husband. I am sorry now, but somehow I think I will be rewarded for helping him through this final dark phase of his life. Maybe I am now fooling myself, but that is how I have to look at this mess.

Well, I am about ready to "call it a day." Hope this message finds you well and putting your life into a positive perspective.

Your friend,
Donna

From: Matty
Sent: Tuesday, August 10, 2004 10:23 AM
To: Donna
Subject: Will write soon

Hi Donna,

I just wanted to let you know that I'm having a few problems with my computer at home, so will write back to you in a few day's time.

If in case you need to reach me for anything, you can still send me an e-mail, and I will be able to check my e-mails through a different computer.

Regards,
Matty

From: Matty
Sent: Wednesday, August 11, 2004 1:47 PM
To: Donna
Subject: Steven De Vore

Hi Donna,

Reading through your e-mail, I'd first like to apologize to you for mentioning the romantic parts of my relationship with Steven. It was not done intentionally, though I understand how it might have given you feelings of jealousy and hurt your self-esteem. I think I would have probably felt the same way as you did.

You mention that the doctors are thinking of performing a "nerve block" for Steven's pain. I don't know what is involved or how they do it, but it does sound a bit risky to me. Would it affect any other parts of his bodily functions? It must be a hard decision to make, whether to remain with painkillers all the time or to go through with such a procedure. Do you know if it's ever been done before and what kind of results were obtained?

Steven also told me about incidents that had happened to him or about things that had happened within the vicinity where he lives, but obviously I had to take his word for it - burst underground pipes with which he helped the municipal workers, sorting out fights between rowdy crowds that were on the property, getting into a physical fight with "Dee's" brother, and many more stories.

Of course as you also said, he too told me that he worked in several jobs - a chef (he had his own restaurant for a while and people raved about his food), worked with the law enforcement, a building contractor, a soldier, a paralegal. He told me how he would help you out with some of your cases, or if "Dee" needed any advice, since she was a lawyer also.

When he came here, he even gave me a ring which he said he received from the law enforcement. I wonder now where he obtained that. I actually forgot to send that back to you too, but will do so at the earliest opportunity.

I found it rather strange that he could do all that seeing as he was "supposedly employed" by the military - but his answer was that although he was an agent, he wasn't always sent out on missions, so it enabled him to work in between his military assignments.

Steven told me that he used to live in Canada, in a small town in the rural areas. There he lived by a river where he often fished (he sent me a picture of one of his big catches). He also took care of a pack of 6 wolves that roamed wild in the surrounding forest area near his home.

He started building and adding on to his home, sometimes single-handedly or sometimes with some help. He managed to do so and had the time for it, because apparently when he had decided to retire from the military a few years earlier, he was called back into service when the Sept. 11 incident happened. He continued working for the military until two years ago.

We had been chatting for about nine months previously, before his "second" retirement, and I think he felt that since meeting me he already wanted to change his "lifestyle" and not risk his life anymore. Although I did not ask it of him, I was mightily relieved that he decided to retire, especially when he would tell me of some of the incidents he was involved in and what risks were on his life. So Donna, you are completely right when you said he knew what "buttons" to push with me. He knew how sorry I felt for him being such a big hero in my eyes, how upset I would get when anything happened to him, and the tears I shed because I took everything to heart.

When he first introduced himself to me, he told me his real name was Steven, and I guess I just got used to calling him that. I never did call him Steve. Since he also told me that he was brought up on an Indian reservation (during the time his grandmother was looking after him) he too was given an Indian name - Wolfwalker. Because he told me that he had such a love for wolves too, when it came to deciding what Jewish name he would choose for himself, I helped him and suggested that he take the name Ze'ev, which means wolf in Hebrew. I think he was pretty satisfied with the choice. I'm only just surprised how you got to know about it if Steven is so concerned about his privacy.

Donna, I too was fooled by Steven with his undying words of love and his promise that he was loyal only to me. What a joke it all seems now. He must have used those words on so many other women and saw the effect and how gullible we all were, and that was the way he managed to charm us all and make us each feel special, so don't feel bad. It seems we were all in the same boat.

I forgot to ask you, was he at least truthful with you that he had been married three times before when you first met?

Although I wrote to you that I may not be able to reply to you for a few days, I've decided to delay fixing up my computer problems till maybe until next week, when I'm more clear about what has to be done. I'll try to let you know in time.

I really admire your sense of responsibility and devotion in taking care of Steven - it can't be easy for you handling two big emotional problems, and my heart goes out to you. I guess although you have felt neglected and unhappy with Steven for so many years, it's not an easy step to take to break up a marriage, especially now that he depends on you even more during this time. I am slowly getting over all that has happened, but the hurt will always be deep inside of me, because I loved him blindly, completely, heart and soul. I just pray to G-d to help you and me and to give me the guidance to overcome the emotional hurdles.

Donna - more power to you.

I wish you all the very best,
Matty

From: Donna Lehl
Sent: Wednesday, August 11, 2004 11:24 PM
To: 'Matty '
Subject: Steven De Vore

Hi Matty,

Steve had the nerve block done today and the doctor feels it was successful and will provide relief for nine to twelve months. I spent from 7:30 this morning until about noon with him and the medical professionals trying to arrange his release from the hospital tomorrow. Then I went to work, worked until about 6:30 p.m.; then I went to the drug store and hardware store to get things he will need when he gets out. I was so exhausted when I finally got home tonight I haven't been able to do anything.

I have to laugh at some of the things Steve told you. Some of them were true or true to a point. The water pipes did break last winter and it did cause a huge hole in the driveway. There were never rowdy crowds at Surfside that I could not handle, but he did like to have everything under very tight control. I used to refer to him as the parking lot police because it used to make him nuts when people did not park in their assigned parking place. I was puzzled about getting into a physical confrontation with "Dee's brother." I can't recall anything even near that happening. He rarely ever saw my brothers

— maybe once a year and my brothers are not the fighting kind. They're not particularly friendly with him, but I've never known of any kind of negative feelings running either way.

As for Dee asking for legal advice from him, it used to annoy me to no end when he thought he could tell me what the law was when lawyers would argue endlessly over what Steve saw in such "black and white" terms. Believe me, the only ones who ever sought legal advice from Steve were the people he lied to about his background and expertise. We talked about him becoming my paralegal, but he never cared to learn anything because he thought he already knew it all.

He did fish a lot when we first came to Surfside. I even spent $6,000 on a boat for him because the one he had was too small for the lake. He did catch a lot of fish, some of them big. I probably took the picture that he sent you. He never did any major building or remodeling, but he did do maintenance on my motel property. I'm sorry I never met his wolves. Lol.

You know for all his sympathy seeking, Steve lived a charmed life. He "guilted" me into buying him whatever he wanted. He didn't have to go to work. All he had to do was mow the grass, remove a little snow in the winter, repair things when they broke and for the most part, his time was his own. He spent most of it reading, watching TV news and the science fiction channel, and talking on the Internet. For a change of pace, I would take him out to lunch or we would go on big shopping trips, often spending several hundred dollars in a day. We went on vacations, although he managed to ruin some part of every trip we took in the past five years by getting insulting, domineering or sulky for part of each trip. He was not happy unless he made me cry in public at least once during every trip.

I'm so happy to hear that you're getting over this betrayal. I am healing as well. I have found that it helps to laugh about the parts of it that are funny, like his wildest stories. My biggest struggle is how to take care of him when I sometimes feel so angry and cheated. Today I found myself wearing down to no energy at all and getting angrier as the day progressed knowing that he would never have done the same for me — he wouldn't even have an honest relationship with me. I wish he had told me two years ago that he had found someone and wanted his freedom. That would have been so much less painful than all this drama and having to cope with his illness. The final blow will be if I get stuck with a bunch of his medical expenses. Well, I am not going to worry about that unless and until I have to.

Well, it's time to walk the dogs and then go to bed. Tomorrow will be a busy day, I'm sure. It will be harder for me to write once Steve gets out of the hospital, because he won't like us writing and he always has to have my undivided attention.

Take care of yourself.

Your friend,
Donna

From: Matty
Sent: Thursday, August 12, 2004 2:18 PM
To: Donna
Subject: Steven De Vore

Hello Donna,

Hope that Steven is feeling better and recovering after having the nerve block done and that it does indeed relieve him of the unbearable pain. How did he take being told that he had pancreatic cancer? The news must have been a terrible blow to him.

Though he didn't show me he was afraid, he was hoping that the biopsy might have resulted in an inflamed pancreas instead which the doctor informed him could be cured over time.

I honestly feel sorry for him. It's not an easy illness for anyone to deal with, nor can it be easy for the immediate family either. I can imagine how tiring and worrisome it is for you too, although you feel angry and cheated. I do hope you'll have some kind of assistance to help you look after Steven. You'll be needing some kind of relief before you wear yourself out.

Donna, I agree with you when you say that Steven lived a charmed life. You supported him for 11 years both emotionally and financially. He didn't work all that time and just took advantage of your good-heartedness, always making you feel guilty in order to get what he wanted out of you, and as far as I can tell, treated you like dirt over time. Didn't you ever find it strange that he had no inclination to work; to help provide and share in expenses? I wonder what sob-story he must have fed you to convince you to support him in such a way (I suppose in an indirect way he did the same to me... which I'll tell you about at a later time). It brings me to think what he was trying to prove when he started this relationship with me, after all, what more could he ask for when he found a comfortable lap to fall on when living with you.

Did it all start off as a joke for him when he first started with me? Was it a game to him? Did he enjoy all this play on my emotions and thought what another foolish woman I was to be taken in by his charms? Believe me, I'm by no means a woman of wealth, nor do I live in a grand apartment, so what was he exactly looking for in me? Some adventure that he played out? An adventure that lasted for 2 ½ years.

I have such conflicting thoughts and emotions about Steven. Putting in a good word for him, and positively speaking, I must say that Steven was always so encouraging towards me, taught me to have some confidence in myself which I was badly lacking, helped me to be strong in my decisions and beliefs, always putting a smile on my face or making me laugh whenever I was worried or feeling low, and at least for that, I thank him. I can thank my lucky stars that I never did see the insulting, domineering or sulky part of Steven's character.

I have always been a very shy and introverted person and he gave me the feeling of being wanted and desired again, to feel important as a person. I can honestly say that I enjoyed chatting with him and getting to know him during those 2 ½ years, even though I now feel a deep hurt at his deceit, but funnily enough I'm not sure I feel any anger. It's more like I feel I should berate myself for being a fool and being blind to his half-truths. I was warned so many times by friends and family to take care, but I guess subconsciously I chose to ignore those warnings.

It was so pleasant chatting with Steven. We spoke on many subjects and discussed many issues. It was enthralling to me and I always looked forward to our daily chats, or whenever it would work out for us to meet online. It's a wonder that you too could not have guessed what Steven was up to when we spent so much time chatting over a long period of time and his excuses for coming twice to Israel.

As for his conversion, I still think it was an admirable thing for him to do, whether for his own sake or mine, and again makes me wonder if he really went through with it with the intention of eventually coming to Israel to live with me. Guess we'll both never know the answer to that, hey? I guess I should also be thankful that everything has come out in the open now... can you imagine if he had started a new life here with me, if in time, he wouldn't have also treated me as he did you. I don't think I would have been able to bear it, and for sure there would have been shouting matches between us, because I will never let anyone insult me in any way, or to embarrass me in public.

Anyway Donna, I understand you won't have much time to write to me once Steven gets back home, and if you prefer I also don't write to you so that Steven doesn't get suspicious about anything, just say so. I'd only like it if you could drop me a line from time to time to let me know how you are both keeping up and how you are managing with everything.

Good luck in all that you do.

My thoughts are with you.

Matty

From: Donna Lehl
Sent: Thursday, August 12, 2004 9:04 PM
To: 'Matty '
Subject: Steven De Vore

Well Matty, the circle is complete. Although not physically in the same room we are all three of us in the same place now. You and I are together through the wonders of modern science and Steven is in a hospital bed six feet away from me. If he is well enough to snoop while I am at work in the days ahead, he will be able to read about our thoughts and how he has cut us both to the core. Somehow, I suspect he will still not really understand what he has done, since he really does think only about himself. I am a bit overwhelmed with his care at the moment, because I feel like I am the only one on whom he can depend and I am not a nurse, yet I am expected to act like one. What really upsets me at the moment is that I am now neglecting my legal work – which is what I am reasonably good at.

I'm glad that your relationship with Steven had some positive benefits for you and that you are now able to see them. I received some positive benefits as well. I have learned for the first time that love is giving, not getting, and for the first time, I really am loving someone else. I really don't expect anything in return for what I am doing for him and I will be satisfied if I get what I expect, nothing.

I have been interested in knowing more about you. How old are you, what do you do, and what do you look like? You know what I look like, you know I am an attorney and you may or may not know that I am 54. I suspect that you are younger because that is what men typically do, dump the old wife for a younger, prettier one? Am I right? Why do you have low self-esteem and a lack of confidence?

I grew up with a father who subscribed to the belief that berating a child is the best way to make them apply themselves. It was true in my case. I have always taken care of myself. I paid my way through college then through law school. I have worked every minute of my adult life, while having and raising two children. In retrospect, I don't know how well I did as a mother, but my kids turned out well, I think. But whatever I do, it is never enough. I was raised Catholic, but I had some issues with the Catholic faith. I raised my children Lutheran (their father's religion) but I never really made a connection with my God or religion, except as an intellectual study, until I studied "A Course in Miracles" and became a part of the Unity church (emphasis upon inclusion of all religions, instead of separation).

So you now know more about me; tell me about Matty.

As a post script, I went to a lot of trouble getting Steve a hospital bed so that he would be comfortable, and so that his bed would be convenient to the TV, kitchen, bathroom and guess what – he has gone into my room and crashed in my bed. I guess I'll have to sleep in the chair. Oh, in a minute I will send you a copy of the e-mail correspondence between Steve and me when he was staying with you the first time. You should find it interesting.

Later,
Donna

From: Donna Lehl
Sent: Thursday, August 12, 2004 9:18 PM
To: Matty
Subject: FW: not hearing from you

Matty, Here is the first message Steven sent me during his first trip to you. You'll see from this and subsequent messages I am sending you what he was up to.

Donna

-----Original Message-----
From: Steven De Vore
Sent: Friday, May 16, 2003 7:56 AM
To: Donna
Subject: Re: not hearing from you

sorry babe been at university of jerusalem and down south they have no
global connect as of yet.. am now at mat's place for the day and took
advantage to get back with you.. will be here all next week..
will send you a follow up of this reply..
love and miss you
steven

From: "Donna J. Lehl" <>
To: <stevendevore@hotmail.com>
Subject: not hearing from you
Date: Wed, 14 May 2003 11:38:27 -0400

Steve,

I am really disappointed that I have only received one very short message from you in ten days. I feel like I must not be very important to you. I think you'd be pretty unhappy if I treated you that way. Do you even care what is happening in my life or that I might be a little worried about you being over there and not hearing whether you're all right? Before you start home, make sure you contact me and tell me you're still coming. If you're not coming back, I don't want to drive to Metro for nothing.

Donna

From: Donna Lehl
Sent: Thursday, August 12, 2004 9:18 PM
To: 'Matty '

Subject: FW: oops

This too from first trip; probably came from your computer while you were out.

Donna

-----Original Message-----
From: Steven De Vore
Sent: Friday, May 16, 2003 8:00 AM
To: Donna
Subject: RE: oops

understand your feelings hunny i could not get to a global workstation upon arrival.. only global workstations are in private sectors like mat's and several other friends here i was real disappointed that i was not able to contact you sooner and sorry i fucked up sending to you on msn.. just got it corrected now and am sending to your hotmail.com

love and miss you

steven

From: "Donna J. Lehl"
To: "'Steven De Vore'"
Subject: RE: oops
Date: Fri, 9 May 2003 16:50:54 -0400

Haven't received a thing from you and was beginning to be very angry that you didn't have the consideration to at least let me know you arrived all right. I cannot get my e-mail from msn.com. I only sent that e-mail to you so that we could chat thru instant messenger if we happened to be on-line at the same time. I love & miss you too, more than you'll ever know, but don't feel like that gives you the right to disrespect me.

Donna

-----Original Message-----
From: Steven De Vore
Sent: Friday, May 09, 2003 1:11 PM
To: Donna
Subject: oops

let me know if you were able to receive last msg i sent to donnalehl@msn.com. if not then will sent anotha
love and miss you

steven

From: Donna Lehl
Sent: Thursday, August 12, 2004 9:19 PM
To: Matty
Subject: FW: all is well

One more from 2003 trip.
-----Original Message-----
From: Steven De Vore
Sent: Sunday, May 18, 2003 4:04 AM
To: Donna
Subject: all is well

donna,

i suppose you heard of the 3 body bombers one that happened yesterday and 2 today.. one was close to where i was going that was the route towards jerusalem university.. missed it by 20 min so thought i ought to turn around and let you know that i am well.. what i was trying to say earlier is that jerusalem university is only online to its local systems in israel it is not global like having an address of www.XXXXX.com and if one would want to get on the world wide web one would need a workstation that has global capacities (i.e., access to www.xxxxx.com instead of being limited to xxxxxx.co.il

anyways the email i sent to wrong address (msn.com) i was saying that there was a delay.. i left detroit one hour later than usual. luggage got to amsterdam okay but amsterdam did not include my luggage on the flight to israel... grrrrrrrrr.. was w/o clean underpants for 5 days.. did not enjoy amsterdam and the 7 hour wait was sorta uncomfortable sure glad i will only have one hour wait coming back :o)

weather here been very hot and dry but have not been out much from computer centre. installing better security system which i once did while working for eds. did a 100 mile southern tour to bar llit university to do same and implement network.

i will be all done with the university thingy by tomorrow or tuesday then i will be working on my friends puters.. having loads of food they feed you well here but darn the humous is starting to give me the case of gas but oh dont i enjoy it hahaha

love and miss you
steven

From: Donna Lehl
Sent: Thursday, August 12, 2004 9:20 PM
To: 'Matty '
Subject: FW: guess you must be out today

Now he's starting to sweat that I won't pick him up at the airport.

-----Original Message-----
From: Steven De Vore
Sent: Sunday, May 18, 2003 12:38 PM
To: Donna
Subject: guess you must be out today

hi hon,

tried to come online to catch you but guess you must either be out visiting or not at puter today.. miss you.

love
steven

From: Donna Lehl
Sent: Thursday, August 12, 2004 9:21 PM
To: Matty
Subject: FW: missing you

Can you believe this crap, Matty?

-----Original Message-----
From: Steven De Vore
Sent: Monday, May 19, 2003 4:16 AM
To: Donna
Subject: missing you

hunny,

oh brother, i have yet to get used to this time difference.. it is 11 am here and you are yet not out of bed.. i miss you so much.. and it will sure be good to get back home and seeing you again..

put in loads of hours and project is about complete and nothing more i cannot do from home whew.

love and miss you
steven

From: Donna Lehl
Sent: Thursday, August 12, 2004 9:23 PM
To: 'Matty '
Subject: FW: still alive and kicking

Matty, this is the last message (I think) that he sent me from Israel during his 2003 trip to you. What a silver-tongued devil.
Donna

-----Original Message-----
From: Steven De Vore
Sent: Tuesday, May 20, 2003 12:26 PM
To: Donna
Subject: still alive and kicking

hunny,

i am still alive and this one was further north west of where i now am. jeruselem project is now complete and the university mainframes are now ready to be connected with their global servers which will be a blessing for those wishing to study online from far off.. all other universities will eventually be connected to the network via jui (jerusalem university of israel). in few hours i will be heading for tel aviv. got connections with a company called merablis.. wanting me to install a security software that will assist them in tracing local middle east hackers that have been paining them badly..

been eating and lodging well and not a penny yet out my pocket. everyone has been super good to me.. hoping to attend to shabbat services at the reform shul here in jerusalem on friday.. keep in mind the customs.. depends on which friend i stay with you may not hear from me until after shabbat..

cannot wait.. will be home as scheduled on sunday unless there is a delay in flight.. sorry to hear the grass did not obey my command (dont over grow until i return)..

alrighty gotta turn over this terminal to mat's rascul as soon as i sent off

an email to my rabbi..

love ya
steven

From: Matty
Sent: Saturday, August 14, 2004 3:40 AM

To: Donna
Subject: Steven De Vore

Hi Donna,

I'm sure you are partly relieved that Steven is home now, less trips to the hospital, but you still have a rough road ahead of you juggling your time between taking care of Steven and attending to your legal work. It's only to be expected that you neglected your work at this time, but I'm sure in the days ahead that things will get back to their normal routine more or less, once Steven becomes a little stronger and less dependant on you and hopefully won't need your undivided attention 24/7.

I don't know what Steven will think if he starts snooping, but I thought you mentioned that you had transferred all our e-mails to each other onto a hard disk and deleted them from your computer. Is there still a way that he can discover that we've been communicating?

I still sometimes find it strange that we have kept up this correspondence - maybe any other woman would have been too hurt to do anything about it and choose to ignore her husband's "fling" but since it seems that we discovered he cheated on both of us, and it was not a one-sided affair, it might seem appropriate that we would both want to know exactly what he was playing at.

I received your other e-mails showing me the letter that you and Steven wrote to each other whilst he was here last year. What can I say Donna? He NEVER did any of those things and I was laughing cynically to myself and felt amazed to see it written in black and white, though that is what you said you were told was the purpose of his visit and meeting up with friends. As I said before, we spent nearly every minute of every day together. There was no way he would have been able to work at computers at the University of Jerusalem (it's not actually called that) nor at any other place. Boy oh boy, what a lot of bullshit he was feeding you. As for the incident with the body-bombers, I only showed him the place where it happened a few months earlier. There were no incidents in the Jerusalem area whilst he was here, at least not anything he could have witnessed.

You said you were interested in knowing more about me. I'm not that much younger than you are - I will be 50 next year. How do I describe myself? I'm petite (5 ft.) have shoulder length auburn hair, wouldn't say I was pretty or stunning, average looks I suppose. So no Donna, in my case Steven did not dump you for a younger and prettier woman. I'll send you a few pictures of me later. I doubt Steven fell for my looks (according to him he had not as yet seen me though my picture was at one time put in a chat album). I think it was more because we had such friendly interesting chats in the beginning and he saw that I was soft-hearted, understanding, and it made no difference to me that he was deaf. I accepted him for what he was - a person with feelings and emotions and not someone to be disdained because of his impairment (he's often told me that people would ignore him when he mentioned he was deaf, which I think might have given him a complex, and was very much a loner).

I've been living in Israel for the past 28 years and have been working in a bank for 27 of those years. I too hope I've been a good mother to my kids. We've had our ups and downs, but which family doesn't? I don't know why I have a low-esteem, it just wasn't easy for me after getting divorced. My children were very small and all my time was spent in taking care of them, working and keeping up with expenses. I really didn't have a social life for many years. I can't say I put myself before them and thinking of meeting up with other men was too much of a frightening thought. I have a very good relationship with my ex-husband, in that he's always seen that we are never in need for anything and a devoted father to his children. He's had a girlfriend for some years now, but he's never neglected his responsibilities towards us. We've just remained very good friends. I consider myself lucky because there are divorce stories that would bring goose bumps to anyone. He on the other hand, I think appreciates the fact that I'm not a materialistic person and have been honest with him throughout everything. I would not intentionally take advantage of any situation and didn't expect any big settlements. I accepted what I got (sometimes I got more than what I expected to get) and therefore our divorce was easier to deal with and have always kept on friendly terms.

I just thank G-d that so far I have

managed with everything, and I believe all that has happened in my life was fated to be for whatever reason it may be.

Thank you for telling me about yourself also. It's admirable that you've always taken care of yourself and succeeded in what you've become and achieved. I pray that things will only get better for you in the future.

Take care as always,
Matty

From: Matty
Sent: Tuesday, August 17, 2004 2:13 PM
To: Donna
Subject: Pictures

Hi Donna,

Here are some pictures I promised to send you. These were taken when Steven came to Israel this year (2004) and a couple of pictures with me and a coworker. I'm the one on the right-hand side with the blue striped T-shirt.

Regards,
Matty

From: Matty
Sent: Wednesday, August 18, 2004 10:53 AM
To: Donna
Subject: Thank you

Dear Donna,

Just wanted to inform you that today I

received your card together with your lovely gift of peace. It was very thoughtful of you to think of me, and your prayers for peace for my country and for my own inner peace are very much appreciated. Thank you so very much. The necklace looks so brand new. I honestly hope you did not go out of your way in buying it especially for me.

I would always laugh and be amazed whenever I received cards from Steven, at how appropriate the meanings written within them were. Things that we would talk about, he would somehow, always find the right card, which I found amusing, so your card too, got a chuckle out of me.

I have not heard from you in a few days, so I hope this e-mail finds you well. I know you said it may be more difficult to write to me once Steven gets home, but I'm sure you must be slowly getting back into things, catching up on all your work, and taking care of everything at home. I understand it can't be easy, and sometimes it seems there are never enough hours in the day to do everything you intended.

Thank you again Donna. I too would like to send you a little souvenir from Israel. If there's anything that you specifically would like to have, please write and tell me.

Warmest regards,
Matty

From: Donna Lehl
Sent: Wednesday, August 18, 2004 10:47 PM

To: 'Matty '
Subject: Steven De Vore

Dear Matty,

I finally got a few minutes to reply to this letter and will try to respond to the others you have sent me since I have been so busy with work, Steve and all.

Steve came home last Thursday and was so bad, in constant pain, Friday that I could not go to work. Luckily he had a visiting nurse in, who was as disturbed as I was to see the condition he was in, and on Saturday she called the doctor and demanded another drug for pain. Because it is a narcotic and the doctor could not call the Rx into the drug store, I had to drive back to the hospital (about 30 miles round trip) just to pick up the Rx and then had to find a drug store to fill it. Luckily it worked at reducing his pain, so it was worth the effort. He has been much better since. He is back to his old self.

We have had a couple of long conversations about his cheating since it came to light and they have not been pleasant. He still insists that you knew he was married and that you only contacted me because he expressed a desire to break it off. He also continues to claim that he took a seminar at the University of Jerusalem this year and that some rabbis paid part of his way. He did finally admit that he had taken money from the motel cash box for the cost of the ticket.

Thanks for the picture, although it did hurt me to see you with him in such a beautiful place. I'm sure you had a great time there together.

He likes to travel and enjoys beautiful scenery. I had made reservations for the two of us to go to Hawaii to visit my son in December, and he asked me yesterday if I was still planning on taking him. I told him I didn't know. When I first found out about his affair, I decided I definitely would not take him. But I have waffled since. I just don't know what to do with us and what is left of our relationship. I ask myself, should I feel nothing, should I enjoy what good there still is? It would be so much easier to just make a clean break.

Steve claims not to have contacted you and to have no interest in doing so, although I told him you wanted to speak with him and I told him that I did not object. He says he took your contact information off his computer. Please let me know if he contacts you.

Funny you have a good relationship with your ex and so do I. We were divorced 17 years ago after 18 years of marriage and after a brief estrangement; we dated each other briefly, then decided we did better as co-parents and friends. We have been friends since before Steve and I got together. He too is a good father and we had a very fair and amicable divorce. He even sent some of his friends to me to get a divorce because I believe in fairness when a couple (especially one with children) splits. He has had a few girlfriends since we separated, but has never remarried. He knows about this thing with Steve and much to my surprise, he wasn't really angry at him. Maybe he knows how these things happen in a man's life.

Well, I need to get ready for bed, so I'd

better say "goodnight." Hope all is well with you.

Best regards,
Donna

From: Matty
Sent: Thursday, August 19, 2004 12:49 PM
To: Donna
Subject: Steven De Vore

Hello Donna,

I'm happy to know for your sake that Steven is back to his old self, but it seems according to what you say that he still lies about some things. I can swear to you Donna, that I never knew he was married and I was even more flabbergasted to know when you told me on the phone that you are his 4th wife. He was so adamant about telling me he was never married.

The only reason I phoned you, was because I was so concerned about Steven's health, not knowing that all this time he was deceiving me. Therefore, I found it strange when I begged Steven several times for your e-mail address or phone number, but he refused to give them to me saying that you were not in the habit of giving such information out. I was not too happy about it, but he reassured me that you (as his "friend") knew about his relationship with me, and if anything came up once he was hospitalized, you would know how to contact me. I assumed he had given you my e-mail address and phone number.

After my last contact with Steven, I saw

that he did not come on-line for a few days and understood that he had been hospitalized which he warned me might be the case if I didn't see him. I was so worried for him, spent endless sleepless nights thinking about what he was going through, and praying to G-d for His help and guidance and to eventually hear that the results of his biopsy would not be as bad as I feared. I was on pins and needles to hear just a word from you about Steven. When 10 days had passed and still no word, I just had to find a way to contact you somehow. My ex-hubby actually helped me discover where you worked and your phone number where you are employed.

Steven did not at all give me any indications that he wanted to break off with me. On the contrary, we ended our last conversation with the usual words of love, that my thoughts would always be with him and how we would be missing each other till the next time we would renew our contact again. Even if he had expressed to me that he desired to break off our relationship, I wouldn't have gone to the trouble of contacting you. It's not in my character to complain to another woman (and especially even if I knew you were his wife). What would it have helped and what benefit would I get out of it? Probably just more heartache. Steven knew that I am the kind of person that would not intentionally step on anyone's toes. When I thought he was on the rebound from his previous relationship and a romantic one was just starting to develop between me and him, I asked him many times if he felt no regrets and maybe wanted to resume his relationship with his ex-girlfriend whom he had also met through the chat (they had not met physically, their only contact too, was just through the internet). He said no, he did not want to go back to her. Ironically, he found out that she had deceived him. She had written a "Dear John" letter to him breaking up their relationship. He had found comfort and love in me, someone that he could trust and valued my honesty.

Donna, he was not in a seminar at the University of Jerusalem, but it makes me think that if he told you some rabbis paid part of his way, that was how he was able to get the rest of the money for his trip here, besides the money he took from the motel cash box. Maybe that is the reason that his rabbi did not reply to you - she might have found out that they were cheated also. Something definitely fishy is going on here. Maybe the rabbinical community there too got word from the University of Jerusalem that Steven never even enrolled for the seminar, but if that is so, it's up to them to follow up on their enquiries.

I understand your indecision about whether to take Steven with you to Hawaii or not. I too would have probably not taken him after finding out that he was having an affair. The thing is that I think I would always feel under some kind of strain despite trying to enjoy what good there still is. It's really a question of how much faith you can put in him. It's so difficult once a person has been hurt to get back the feeling of trust they once had. Maybe, just maybe now, Steven is showing the inclination to prove to you that he wants things to be as before when you first met, and to make it up to you before his nastiness and domineering ways became apparent to you.

Donna, I don't know what to advise you nor is it my place to tell you what to do. You have to trust your own feelings and instincts in this matter. I know it's not an easy decision to make and probably feel torn in whatever you decide. As long as you feel whole with yourself afterwards, that will be good.

As for Steven claiming not having contacted me - that's true enough. I have not received a word from him. I have not as yet taken his contact information off my computer in the hopes that I would still be able to have a chance to talk to him one last time. What I wanted to mention though, was that one evening during this week whilst sitting on the computer I saw him coming on-line. (I nearly flipped) I waited to see if he would contact me, not knowing that he had taken my name off his list of contacts. When he didn't, I tried to get through to him. At that moment, I didn't know whether to do so or not, but decided to go through with it. He was on-line for maybe 5 minutes or so and did not reply to me, then he went off-line.

I've been thinking about it, but as yet undecided whether to send him an e-mail. For all I know, he may decide not to open it and just delete it from his files. Would you really mind though if I did confront him with all he's done? I will of course not mention that we've been e-mailing each other. I just want to refer more to the fact of what happened between me and him and how I feel about it all. I doubt I'll get any replies from him, but if I don't try, I won't know.

By the way, as for the coasters he brought for you from Israel - that was supposedly a gift to you from Sarah. He must have bought them whilst we were on one of our shopping sprees. I feel I really want to give you a gift that's from me. You are quite right when you said that our e-mail exchanges could be therapeutic for us... in a way I feel that it has lightened the burden for me talking it all out. I feel less in the dark, as we share our mutual experiences we have or had (in my case) with regard to Steven, but the hurt will always remain with me.

I did wear your peace sign necklace you sent to me, and got many compliments for it. Thank you again Donna, and for just being there for me, despite the weird connection that has developed between us. I feel that you are the kind of person that is fair and understanding. I hope I'm right in my thoughts about you.

Hope to hear from you again soon, whenever you have the time.

Best regards,
Matty

From: Donna Lehl
Sent: Tuesday, August 24, 2004 8:46 PM
To: 'Matty '
Subject: Steven De Vore

Hi Matty,

Sorry it has taken me so long to get back

to you, but as I anticipated, I have little or no time to myself and when I do, it is away from home, out with my friends.

I took your suggestion, or rather your question to me about whether I had ever tried to contact Steve's other wives. It led me to try finding them. While we were up north this past weekend I found the name of the wife before me. I did a Google search and found someone I suspected was her. I e-mailed her and today she called me. At first she seemed a little nervous and tentative, but then she seemed genuinely relieved to know that there was someone else gullible enough to be taken in by him. She began our conversation (after she verified that I was who I said I was) by saying that she was married to Steven for 3 years and what she knows about him is that he is a "mental case and dangerous." She claims he was physically abusive to her, tried to burn her with a cigarette lighter among other things. About his propensity for prevarication, she said he was "a professional fabricator." Apparently you and I were luckier because he was never physically abusive to us. Interestingly enough, I felt a sort of kinship with her as well. We have similar personalities and even worked in the same field, more or less. She really wants to meet face to face and says that she has many times thought about writing a book about Steven – sort of a cautionary tale, warning signs you are being courted by a con type book (my interpretation of what she was saying, not her words, exactly). Anyway, it was very interesting. She may lead me to other wives and girlfriends to round out my cast of characters.

Now, for a response to your message: Of course I do not mind if you e-mail Steve. I have no delusions that his newfound amorousness has more to do with his need for someone to care for him than my charm. I think he should have to face your feelings. Getting it second hand from me isolates him from the responsibility for the pain he caused you and allows him to continue his charade (although I am no longer fooled by any of it).

Matty, please understand that when I report to you what Steven says about you — that you knew he was married and he tried to break it off and you contacted me to spite him — I do not believe one single word of it. Our first telephone call told all for me. If all that he said was true, you should be given an academy award for acting. And besides, as a lawyer, I have been trained to ask in these situations "who has the motive to lie" and "who has a known character for dishonesty?" We both know the answer, all too well. So, please, do not concern yourself with having to prove your character to me. I think I know you fairly well because we are "cut from the same cloth."

Steve told me about seeing you come online and that he ignored your invitation to talk. Funny but wife number three and I were talking about the same thing today. That occasionally he tells the truth, which makes it easier to believe the lies.

I guess I will take him to Hawaii with me if he is able to travel in December because the airline has told me that the ticket is nontransferable. We used to have such fun on vacations, back when I think he really did love me and we seemed to like the same things. This trip, if it happens, will be more like a "farewell tour."

I don't know that Steve's rabbi has contacted him yet, but several members of the congregation have sent him get well cards.

Health report: he's had two doses of chemo and today he had a port installed so that they do not have to put an IV in him each time. We went up north Saturday and came back Sunday. He seemed okay, but it all seemed to tire him out.

I am so glad that you are enjoying the peace sign necklace. When Steven came home from the hospital, he put his jewelry back on, the chain and wedding ring from me and the chain and Star of David from you. Apparently they all still mean something to him.

Hope all is well with you.

Fond wishes,
Donna

From: Matty
Sent: Saturday, August 28, 2004 5:17 AM
To: Donna
Subject: Steven De Vore

Hiya Donna,

I understand that you are keeping pretty busy, but happy to know that at least you are going out with friends which probably helps give you some sort of break from all that you have to deal with at this time. As for me, I rarely go out. I've fallen into some kind of lethargy where I just don't feel like doing anything. My friends and family are a great support to me and try to persuade me every now and then to go out just for a change of scenery. I did that last weekend and spent a day at the beach, which I hadn't done in a long while. It was so calm and soothing for me and I had a wonderful time. I'm now working on myself to try and take each day as it comes and to enjoy the good things in life, to stop moping and try to cease thinking about Steven and the deep hurt I feel.

I appreciate the fact that you believe in my honesty, but had to smile that you've mentioned twice now I would make a good actress if in fact I was lying. No Donna, that's just not me. I don't see the point in lying. Maybe for Steven it was all a thrilling game in his life, but eventually one does get caught out, with usually unpleasant results as can be shown by what happened to us. Unfortunately, his deceit has affected and touched to the core the emotional feelings of those he has been in contact with, or with whom he's been close.

I admire the fact that you've been able to contact wife No. 3. It must have been a very interesting conversation, probably finding out more things about Steven that you weren't aware of. It kind of jolted me though to read that he has an abusive streak in him, but I guess I shouldn't be too surprised since in our chats together he would sometimes show his anger at someone or something that had happened and would state his vengeance for "pay-backs." This would scare me, and often I would calm him down. Ironically he would get like this when someone on the chat would mention, by the way, that she had an abusive experience, or even if I mentioned that I had some sort of disagreement with my ex-hubby, he would get so upset and start swearing like a trooper. I thought that these shows of his violent moods were from his harsh "military" days, where he was usually put in danger and risking his life. Or if something didn't go his way or being hen-pecked by "Dee," he would tell me that he needed to get to Donna to sort the situation out. It sounds so absurd now, especially in the light of what wife No. 3 told you about his abusiveness towards her. So yes Donna, I agree with you that we were very lucky not to have seen this side of him.

Anyhow it would be interesting if you do meet up with her and discover any more things from his previous marriages and romances too. I understand the kinship you might have felt towards her, after all, weren't we all in the same boat? I guess when someone has been through the same experiences a kind of bond develops somehow, and the need to share the emotional pain is dominant. Seems to me that you are both serious about writing a book about your individual experiences. My youngest daughter too has written a rough layout and is trying to convince me to get it in print to warn others not to be fooled by such cons. I'm not sure yet if I'm prepared for that though.

Anyway, how is Steven doing now

after having the nerve block procedure done? Is it helping him to have less pain and be less dependant on the large amounts of narcotics he was taking? I suppose it's too early to know what effect the chemo has on him also. I'm sure your trip up north must have been a good change for him. I hope it was just as pleasant for you too.

As for Steven putting his jewellery back on, I guess he must still appreciate something in the both of us.

Looking forward to hearing from you soon.

Take care as always,
Matty

From: Donna Lehl
Sent: Friday, September 03, 2004 8:16 PM
To: 'Matty '
Subject: RE: Steven De Vore

Hi Matty,

Sorry it's been so long since I wrote, but as I anticipated, working, taking care of Steve and dealing with all the stuff that comes up as a long-distance motel proprietor has left me with very little free time. I did manage to get away for 24 hours to make an out-of-town business trip, which sort of returned me to my normal life and gave me some comic relief with a good friend who also went with me. Funny thing, she is young enough to be one of my kids, but we always have such fun together – we just seem to have the same weird sense of humor I guess.

I have what I hope is a serious prospect to purchase my motel. He wants to see it for the third time this weekend, which for us is a long holiday weekend. I am praying things work out and he decides to buy since it will significantly reduce my worries to be rid of it.

I am also giving serious consideration to buying a little house near where I work since it is such a waste, I think, to give money to someone else for the privilege to live where you will never have an ownership interest. The second house I saw I liked very much. Steve also liked it and is encouraging me to buy it. It just makes me a little nervous to buy without having a thorough knowledge of what is currently available, but on the other hand, I don't have much time or energy to shop.

I finally had contact with Steve's rabbi, but she did not contact me directly because for some reason she never got my e-mail message. She called the spiritual services department of the hospital Steve was in and they called me asking if I would contact her. She was concerned about him because no one had heard from him in quite a while and the last they knew he was not feeling well. I called her back and – you guessed it – she was surprised to learn that he was married, at least to someone locally. All she knew is that he had "family" in Israel. She asked me if he did in fact have family there and I said – only his mistress and her family. She was shocked that we had been married for almost 8 years. She did confirm that he had converted and told me that I would have been welcome to participate in the ceremonies if Steve had not discouraged me from being involved. She confirmed that she was married last year shortly after Steve came back from Israel. She said she didn't know of any paramours at the shul, said one female there took a platonic interest in him.

Well Steve has taken his fourth dose of chemo and it's funny but right after he is raring to go, wants to eat, gets around pretty well. But about 4-6 hours later, and for about 24 hours, he is pretty strange – sleeps sitting up, wanders the house all night, can't remember things. Then he gradually seems to get better until it's time for the next dose. He is down to 156 pounds (not sure of the conversion to kilos). He is now officially underweight for his height.

Well, I gotta go. I've got some things I must get done tonight. Take care and keep in touch.

Your friend,
Donna

From: Donna Lehl
Sent: Thursday, September 09, 2004 7:50 AM
To: 'Matty '
Subject: Steven De Vore

Matty, I haven't heard from you since I responded 9/3/04. Since Steve is up and around while I am out, it occurred to me that he might try to put a stop to our communication by intercepting and deleting your messages to me. Therefore, to the extent you want to communicate with me in the future, I think it best you write me at lehld@pepperlaw.com (my work address).

Have a lovely day,
Donna

Chapter Five

When Things Are Ready to Change, They Will

I made the "Michigan Left" onto Shoreline, a term every Michigander understands to mean making a left turn on a divided street by passing your street, getting to the far left, making a U-turn, and then backtracking before turning right onto the desired street. Probably every state has them and people there probably call them an "Ohio Left," a "Texas Left," etc. I didn't actually think about the turn since I don't think I actually was thinking about anything. I was just cruising on autopilot as I seemed to do more and more lately. Whole weeks would go by without so much as an acknowledgment from me of their passing. I hadn't been much into "smelling the roses" since Steve came home from the hospital.

I thought that it would be easier when I didn't have to drive to Royal Oak every night after work to see him in the hospital. But now there were new chores to perform. I had to see that he had all of his medicines – a moving target, since the doctors were still trying to fine-tune the medication regimen that would control the pain, keep the blood sugar regulated, keep the colon performing, and keep him from falling into a deep depression. I had to manage his schedule that included appointments with three doctors, a variety of visiting nurses, and weekly chemotherapy. I had to try to get him to eat something. One week it was soups and homemade juices, the next it was fortified beverages, then it was M&M's and Vernors ginger ale. Whatever Nurse Carol suggested, I would have to obtain and make sure that it was handy for him so he would be encouraged to eat.

Still, he continued to lose weight. At his largest he had weighed 276 pounds. After last year's diet, he had reached a svelte 175. As soon as I went to the city to work and he was cooking for himself again, his weight crept back up to 212, which is about what he weighed this past April when he went to see Matty the last time. At his last chemotherapy appointment, he weighed 156 pounds. He had lost about 35 pounds in four months. His skin hung on him like a bad suit on a wire hanger. He had cried, sobbing wildly, when he caught sight of himself while drying off after a shower in the hospital. Since then I tried to keep him away from mirrors, because it was getting worse every day. It horrified me to see how quickly a body could melt away, leaving just skin and bones.

I stopped at the mailbox bank as I did automatically every day and emptied the box of its contents, placing the pile of bills and junk mail on the seat beside me. I spotted the Beachwood Townhomes return address right away and opened the envelope before pulling away from the mailboxes. The letter was brief and to the point.

"Your current lease expires October 31, 2004. Your renewal lease rate will be $1,050.00. If you plan to move at the end of the current lease period, you must let the office know of your plans on or before August 31, 2004."

Man, that only gave me two weeks to decide if I was going to stay or move. I hadn't even been looking and I wasn't sure if I could get a loan with no down payment. But the apartment was way too small for two people, two dogs, and a bunch of medical equipment. I really should get out of here, I thought. I just hated throwing money away on rent.

I had rented the apartment with the idea that I would bunk there during the week and return home to Tawas every weekend. But I needed to sell the motel to be in a position to buy a home. I had been trying to sell it, without success, for five years. Another listing agreement, with the fourth realtor, had just ended. Like all of the others, he tried at the last minute to get a prospective purchaser to look at the property so that it would seem as though he'd be able to sell it. After all this time, I'm not so sure anyone can sell it, least of all this guy. He had shown the property only a few times in the 18 months he had the listing. I thought about trying to sell it myself on eBay. My brother Darrell loved to buy and sell on eBay, so maybe he could help me set up an account.

But the more immediate problem would be buying a house, even if I could get financing. It seemed impossible that I could find something and move before the beginning of the new lease term.

"Go for it, babe!" Steve said when we discussed the possibility of moving out of the one-bedroom apartment that evening. "Let's get a nice little place with a yard so the dogs can go outside on their own."

That night I began searching the Internet for houses within a 25-mile radius of Detroit in the $125,000 to $200,000 range. I knew the kind of location I wanted – a stable old neighborhood with brick homes and lots of trees, or maybe one of the so-called hip, new cities. But the house had to be a ranch since a hip replacement now seemed to be a matter of when, not if. Lots of stairs would be out of the question.

While on-line, I checked out eBay and to my surprise, saw that they accepted real estate listings. On a lark, I listed the motel for sale. I started a list of houses to view. I made a note to call the mortgage company that financed my house on the lake before I bought the motel.

The next morning, I called my contact at Rock Financial and learned that not only would they lend me $150,000 to $200,000 with no down payment, they would give me an interest-only loan for a period of years.

"Hmm," I mused, "I guess I can pull this off after all."

The following week I surfed the net each night, printing off house listings and map-questing their locations. On Sunday morning I poured over the real estate section of the Detroit Free Press and decided to go check out some open houses. Steve went along, but as soon as we got to the first house, he groaned sleepily and told me to go look and let him know if it was something I thought he should look at, meaning did I like it enough to consider buying.

We started in Saint Clair Shores, a bedroom community bordering Lake St. Clair. It was an established community where most of the houses were three-bedroom brick ranches built in the 1950s. The lawns were well-manicured, the streets were tree-lined and even on weekends, it was quiet. There was a freeway to Detroit running through it and lots of restaurants and shopping.

The third house I looked at was the one. The yard was attractive and when I walked through the front door, I stepped into a wide-open, well-decorated living room, dining area and kitchen with shiny oak floors and an attractive kitchen with plenty of cabinets. Wow, I thought, even the décor looked like something I would have planned. The owners were cordial and began the tour: a full tile bath, a guest room, and a master bedroom with plush burgundy carpet. The master bedroom had originally been two rooms, so it was twice as large as one would expect in these houses. It had two large closets and room for lots of furniture. It would hold all of my new furniture, and then some. A half bath was located between the bedroom and the kitchen, next to the door to the outside, and the stairs to the basement. As I continued the tour, I tried not to let them see my growing excitement. If they knew how much I wanted it, I would be at a disadvantage when the negotiations began.

By the time I got a glimpse of the finished basement, I knew I wanted Steve to see it, but I continued on the owner's pre-planned tour. Still trying not to act excited, I picked out the room for my office, started mentally arranging furniture, and imagined the entertaining I could do. On the way to the back yard and garage, I asked if I could go get my husband for the rest of the showing.

"This is it, Steve. It's perfect," I said. "You'd better come look at it if you feel able."

He got out of the car with an exaggerated effort. Sometimes, I thought, he looked like he just wanted sympathy. He was probably just fine when I wasn't watching him. He made his way up the single step with his cane on one side while I lifted him on the other. He weakly extended his claw-like hand to greet the man of the house and smiled with his lips closed. He never showed his teeth when he smiled. He was self-conscious about his worn and yellowed teeth. He claimed his incisors were worn flat from eating lemons and limes picked off the tree when he was a child. I had never heard of such a thing, but that didn't mean it hadn't happened. Only now that I knew he was a liar, I doubted every strange thing he had ever told me. He nodded his head in a kind of greeting as I explained to the owners that he was not well and deaf, and so he didn't usually speak much when he first met people.

We went through each room of the upstairs again, out into the yard, and the one and a half-car garage. He gazed down the basement steps and questioned whether it was fully finished. He also asked if the house had air conditioning by forming the sign language letters – AC followed by a question mark drawn in the air. I shook my closed fist up and down – the sign for "yes." Although we didn't sign to each other much because I could understand his speech and he could read my lips quite well, it was a skill that came in handy when we wanted to talk in front of others without being overheard.

I was heading for the door and thanking the homeowners for showing us the house and yard a second time, when Steve unexpectedly sat down at their dining table. My initial irritation turned to concern when he tiredly ran his hand across his face. The homeowners and I sat down with him.

He began to speak in a quiet voice, enunciating as well as he could. "I'm dying. I have cancer. The doctor gives me six months to live. I want my wife to have a nice little house she can take care of with a yard for my dogs. We like your house. What will you take for it?"

The homeowners looked at Steve, clearly shocked by his announcement, and then they looked back at me quizzically. I wasn't sure if they were wondering if what he said was true or whether he was going to draw his last breath in their dining room.

I was really irritated now, but I tried to hide it by smiling at the homeowners in a reassuring way. I had planned not to let them know how much we liked their house at this stage. I wanted to look at some other houses for comparison and then call them to to take a second look in a couple of weeks. Maybe in the meantime I would have thought of some things that could use improving, were missing or that needed updating so that I could broach the subject of a reduced price. I could feel my bargaining power seeping away.

"Okay honey, I think it's time we got you home and I bet these folks would like to eat dinner," I said.

I helped him up with a bit more force than necessary and got him out the door and down the step. Then I went back to thank the owners again and to find out when they could give me possession if I decided to buy the house.

When I returned to the car, Steve was standing by the door and a little girl with long red curls was holding open the passenger side door.

"I'm helping your grandpa get into the car," she said.

I couldn't control my laughter as I loaded Steve and then myself into the car. Of course he wanted to know what that kid was doing and what she had said. He was not amused when

I told him what she had said. I couldn't help thinking though that he had received his "just dues" for having told me several times, when my hair was white (before I colored it to escape blatant age discrimination) that people who met us together thought that I was his mother. He would laugh, stroke his still-thick dark hair and call me "mom."

"So, why on earth did you tell those people you are dying?" I asked him when we got back to the apartment and sat at the table where he could more easily read my lips.

"I knew they would feel sorry for us and they would take less for the house. And besides, I **am** dying," he said, looking at me with tears welling up in his eyes. "You'll be rid of me soon."

I didn't know what to feel. Should I be sad, feel sorry for him, be angry because he was obviously seeking my pity? I hugged him but still could not identify how I felt. It was a sort of numbness, like I had been injected with Novocain. I knew there was pain underneath, but it was masked by something unknown.

He spoke quietly, his voice muffled against my breast, "I love you very much."

"Yeah, right," I felt myself say automatically.

I didn't look at him so he couldn't read my lips. But he could probably sense my words from the feel of the air escaping my lungs and the vibration of my chest as I spoke.

We looked at other houses over the next couple of weeks. We contacted three realtors, all of whom had been recommended by friends, and took daylong viewing trips with each. We liked other houses, but each one had something wrong — too much road noise, a crack in the basement wall, kitchen was too small, or the neighborhood seemed to be in transition and not in a good way. The "hip" cities of Ferndale and Royal Oak cost too much and all of the houses were bungalows with second-story bedrooms. The best house was the first house. No matter what we looked at, it seemed to stick in my mind.

After three weeks, Steve and my mind wouldn't quit nagging – just make an offer. If it was meant to be, it would happen. I wanted to pay no more than $150,000 for a house, since I knew that the payment on that amount would be about what I'd been paying for the apartment. The owners were asking $163,000. I made an appointment to meet with them to discuss the purchase further.

I offered $140,000, but was careful to explain the reason for the lowball offer was my own financial situation, not the value of the home. I complimented them on the way they had maintained and improved the condition of the home. I apologized for not being able to pay more. I used my best Dale Carnegie skills to make them want to come to the table. They said they would think about it. That was all I could ask.

There was a message from them on my answering machine before I could drive the eight miles back to the apartment. Could I pay $150,000? That was the least they could take to recover their investment. That was my number. I took it as a sign that the deal was meant to be.

So now, in addition to working full time, and providing primary care and medical transportation to my dying husband, I began planning for the move. I decided there was little in the Tawas City home that was worth moving; it was all old and had suffered "pet abuse." I could move the new bedroom outfit and dining set I purchased for the apartment and the leather chair that served as my only living room furniture, but I would need a sofa and maybe a love seat to fill the living room.

Although he was having a hard time getting around, Steve insisted on shopping for furniture with me. He would hobble into the furniture stores using his cane on one side while I provided support on his other side. He would find a "wheeling chair," as he called them, in the handicap-friendly stores and would hop in, waiting for me to push him to the living room department. He got up and sat in every love seat that was also a recliner. He knew what he wanted. He wanted a recliner so that I could put my aching legs up. He wanted a love seat so we would have to sit close together, close enough so we could touch. He wanted to hold my hand and watch television together.

"I love you," he would say every time we tried out another love seat.

"Yeah, right," I would always reply.

It was kind of a ritual. He tried to make up for his affair and a part of me tried to punish him for it.

Eventually we found a navy blue, leather, reclining love seat for us and a burgundy leather sofa (for company). A multi-colored floral rug would pull together the contrasting colors. The store would hold our purchases until our move.

***

Labor Day weekend approached and I decided to return to the motel for the weekend to honor reservations made months before when Steve was still running the business. It would be a chance to catch up with friends who had been shocked to see the motel suddenly closed with a sign on the door reading: "Closed indefinitely due to family emergency. For information, call: 586-792-XXXX." I had received a few calls from local merchants and regular motel patrons. I told them Steve wasn't feeling well and that I had brought him down to the city to obtain medical care. I hadn't told anyone that it was pancreatic cancer and that it was terminal. Only a few people at work knew about Matty and that was how I wanted it to stay as long as he was alive. His life was miserable enough. I didn't want my family and friends to hate him too.

He made the trip well enough, talking and seeming to enjoy the familiar sights.

"I think I can drive my truck back," he said. "I won't use it much, but maybe I can go to the grocery store or pick up my own medications."

"We'll see how you feel at the end of the weekend." I said, while thinking that it could not be good to drive under the influence of fentanyl and morphine. But when was the last time he listened to me?

It was good to be back in Tawas and although I had discovered that a view of the bay was NOT worth half the pay, it really was a lovely little town with lots of friendly people. Tawas was actually two small towns, nestled side by side along the picturesque Lake Huron shoreline. Tawas City was the county seat, the center of government services, and home to the only hospital in a 40-mile radius. East Tawas was more tourist-friendly, with a large dock, the Holiday Inn Hotel, many "mom and pop" resorts, and a three-block downtown full of fudge shops, restaurants, and up-north gift shops. The two cities shared a school system and a police department, but they jealously refused to join other government functions, even though it was nearly impossible to tell where one ended and the other began. Visitors usually just referred to the area as "Tawas" and were surprised to learn that there were actually two cities.

I visited with next-door neighbors Jim and Joan, with whom Steve refused to speak since a disagreement three years earlier, and I spent time with my friend Jane, who had been battling uterine cancer for many years, and her husband Jerry. I reluctantly told them about Steve's condition, but was careful to tell Jane that pancreatic cancer was nothing like uterine cancer from which she might someday recover. Jane didn't need any kid-glove handling though. She was one tough cookie. She refused to give up and she wouldn't feel sorry for herself. She always expressed gratitude even though the economy had closed their auto repair business, she didn't have medical insurance, and their finances were dismal. I had learned a lot about happiness from Jane. It wasn't about how you feel or what you have. It was all about what you could do for someone else. One time Jane and I had been at a craft show and one of the vendors shivered in the cold wind blowing off Lake Huron. Jane went two booths down the row of crafters, purchased a fleece throw with her last ten dollars and took it back to the vendor, whom she had never met. She believed in karma and she knew that by giving to others she assured that she would continue to have what she needed, just in time.

I also called my fellow motel proprietor and friend Jean, with whom I had served on the controversial tourist bureau board. We had bonded in the face of a chasm that had torn apart the organization and nearly caused it to disband. Jean and her husband John had signed a contract to sell their motel to be razed for the construction of more condominiums along the lake, and none too soon. John had recently suffered a stroke that left him unable to clean and maintain the rooms, and Jean had been forced to leave her job to run the motel.

"Boy, I wish I could get lucky and find a buyer!" I told Jean.

"Hmm, I hadn't thought about your place," Jean said. "I have some customers here this weekend that are looking at resorts to buy. They wanted lakefront, but they just told me all the places they looked at were either run-down or they couldn't afford them. If they're in their room, I'll go down there and talk with them about your place. It may be just what they're looking for."

"I really appreciate that, Jean. I need to unload this place soon because it doesn't look like Steve will be able to come back up here to run the place and my job is way too good to leave. I've been feeling really desperate to sell. I even listed the place on eBay!"

"That's pretty funny," Jean chuckled. "I heard they'd sell

anything, but I would have never thought of listing a business for sale on eBay. So I'll talk to Don and Becky and see if they want to have a look."

"Thanks Jean, take care of yourself and John, and make sure to let me know your new address after you find a place to move."

I hung up the phone and headed to the kitchen to whip up a little light dinner. I opened the freezer to see what we had left there but quickly found myself gazing out the front window instead, admiring the reflection of one of those early fall sunsets that turn bright blue to pink and purple in a matter of minutes. I finally closed the freezer door to devote all of my attention to the sky and the duplication of the sky on the water.

"What a beautiful place," I said out loud. "It's too bad I can't make a living here."

Before I could open the freezer again, I heard the unmistakable sound of motorcycles, a couple of them, in the driveway. Business, I thought, while making the cha-ching gesture. Yes! Maybe I'll rent that last room. I opened the hand-painted glass door and stepped back behind the Dutch door, waiting for the man and woman in leather to step inside the entryway.

"Hi there, how're you folks tonight?" I asked.

"We're fine," said the large, bearded, biker-type guy with a long ponytail as he pulled off his helmet. "I'm Don and this is my partner Becky and we've been staying at the Martins, and Jean over there just told us you had a motel for sale that we should look at before we go back to Traverse City. Would you mind letting us look around?"

Although my initial reaction was to think that this biker and his blond "biker mama" didn't look much like motel proprietors, I remembered what Steve and I looked like when we were motel shopping. That was during Steve's Sioux identity days, when he wore his hair long and had me braid it, either two braids, one on each shoulder or a single braid down the middle of his back. And I never looked like a lawyer unless I was on my way to court. When I wasn't working, I always wore jeans and t-shirts and no make-up. The fanciest car I ever drove was a Toyota Celica, the celebration of my freedom from hauling my children around, when the kids got their licenses and their first cars. The bikers, however, had two brand-new Harleys, each of which I computed was worth more than our two used Toyotas combined.

I gave them the tour: the nine motel units, the storage and service areas, the fish cleaning station, the river, located way down below the nine, now unused, docks, the 180 feet of highway frontage, and the beautiful, uncluttered view of Tawas Bay. I could have given the tour in my sleep. I had shown it dozens of times in the five years it had been on the market. It had been listed with several realtors and they normally would let me show it since I couldn't stand back and let them do it without getting involved. I knew the property's strengths and its weaknesses, and how to showcase or minimize as the case might be. The lawyer in me was always careful not to promise or guarantee, and to qualify any opinion.

The house was last. We had done some updating, but it needed more. I apologized for the messiness and explained that I had been living "downstate" for a year and my husband had been staying there alone, running the motel until he became ill and joined me in the city. Don and Becky were quiet while going through the house and politely thanked me for letting them see the property without any warning. They'd think about it and let me know if they had any questions. Yadda, yadda, yadda, I thought.

They left and I thought we had seen the last of them. They were probably turned-off by the low water or the lack of lake frontage, although I had always been of the opinion that the property had the best of both worlds. The thin strip of land on the lake directly across from the motel was owned by the city and was zoned for public recreation. Nothing would ever be built on it and rarely did anyone except Surfside's customers use the beach there. Therefore, I had all of the benefits of lake frontage without the tax bill.

Steve was feeling pretty well all weekend and he enjoyed puttering around the yard and the garage, and visiting with friends. He fired up his 12-year-old Toyota pickup and drove it to the party store for a bottle of wine to go with dinner. When it came time to leave on Monday morning, he told me he thought he could handle driving it back to the apartment so he would have his own transportation and we would also have it for the upcoming move. He "sealed the deal" by telling me that he had only taken Motrin for pain that morning, and he wouldn't take the strong stuff until he got home that evening. I reluctantly agreed and we loaded the truck with stuff I had been wishing we had, but never had room to bring back. We planned to drive the 40 miles to Standish and then stop for lunch at Wheeler's Restaurant.

I pulled out, heading south on US 23 and Steve followed. I watched him driving in the rearview mirror and mumbled to myself each time I saw him cross the center line— "Man, I hope he's going to be okay."

Finally we rounded the bend just outside of downtown Standish and I pulled into Wheeler's parking lot, leaving the handicapped spot closest to the door for Steve to pull in behind me. That handicapped permit had been helpful since I often had to run ahead and find him a wheelchair at the cancer center, or I had to walk with him until we could find a motorized cart. And, of course, I had my own issues with being able to walk long distances.

I met him at the truck door and helped him out, to the front of the restaurant and up the front steps. He almost couldn't pull himself up the three steps and into the door. The sign said "Please Seat Yourself." We took the first booth, closest to the door.

We ordered lunch and were sitting there people-watching when Steve announced quietly and sort of sheepishly: "I don't think I can make it to the apartment. I almost didn't make it here. I'm not even sure I can take the truck back to Tawas."

"Greaaaat." I said, drawing out the word beyond any necessity. So what the fuck are we supposed to do now? I thought. I mumbled some more under my breath, while Steve stared into his coffee. He had learned a long time ago to avoid my agitation with him by simply looking elsewhere. This maneuver sometimes made me all the more irritated, because I had no such simple escape hatch. I just had to deal with it, whatever IT was.

"It'll be all right," I said, patting his hand reassuringly. "Eat your lunch. I have an idea."

Jerry answered the phone and it was obvious they had caller ID because instead of saying "hello," he said "I thought you left hours ago."

"We did, but we're in Standish and Steve can't go any farther. How would you guys like to come down with us, have dinner, stay the night or whatever, all on me? I just need one of you to drive Steve's truck down to Harrison Township."

"Let me ask Jane," he said. "When do you need us to meet you?"

"Whenever you can get here," I answered.

Jerry and Jane pulled into the parking lot in Jane's red Chrysler LeBaron, aka "The Red Baron," about an hour later. I waited for them to come in and asked them if they wanted to eat before they got on the road.

"Nah, let's get this show on the road," Jane said. "I'd like to get back before midnight because I have a doctor's appointment tomorrow afternoon."

"Are you sure you're okay to do this? It's a pretty long drive. It's at least two and a half hours from here."

"I'm fine. I just don't want to be on the road too late."

"You're too much, Jane," I said. "I don't know what I'd do without you guys," I said as I hugged my good friend.

"No biggie" said Jane, following Jerry out the door and down the stairs. By the time I got Steve up, out the door and to the parking lot, Jerry had adjusted the seat and mirrors on the truck and was trying to figure out how to disengage the emergency brake.

"I thought I fixed this damn thing!" He grumbled.

"You did, it's just temperamental," I said. "I don't know why he insists on using the emergency brake when he parks on a flat surface, but that's another story."

The trip back to the city was uneventful although excruciatingly long with the holiday traffic. Steve was asleep before we reached I-75. I cranked up the music and thought again, as I had many times, that there were definite benefits to being married to a deaf man. I could always listen to what I wanted to listen to and he didn't know unless it was loud enough for him to feel or unless he had been trying to get my attention and I was unresponsive.

"Do you have the stereo playing?" He'd shout, clearly agitated. I remembered finding CDs in his truck when we were dating and asking him whose they were. "They're mine. Sometimes when I'm alone, I listen to music. I listen by feeling it."

That explained the heavy metal, I remembered thinking at the time.

I also recalled the time we were doing the tourist thing on Bourbon Street in New Orleans. We were poking around the T-shirt shop in an old frame building and the Cajun music was rattling the windows and vibrating the floor. I was bouncing involuntarily to the music and Steve was playing the air drums.

We were laughing uproariously at each other.

"Buy that CD," he ordered.

I complied and bought three more while I was at it. They came in handy when we were hosting Mardi Gras at the Trailhead, an annual charity event to raise money to groom and maintain the local cross-country ski trails. We had some great times on vacation and a nice life together in Tawas, for as long as it lasted. The present reality crept back into my consciousness.

We arrived home in one piece. I unloaded the truck with Jerry's help, sent Jerry and Jane on their way, walked the dogs, and tucked Steve into the hospital bed that now formed the divider between the living and dining rooms of the small one-bedroom apartment. He normally insisted on sleeping in the bedroom with me, but tonight he was sleeping sitting up in his clothes. I was just barely able to get his shoes and jacket off, and he didn't fight me leading him the few feet to the open bed.

"You can rest here, while I read my e-mail." I looked at him as I spoke slowly, making sure he was looking at me. I changed the fentanyl patch on his arm, gave him a shot of insulin, and made note of the patch application in his journal. Then I settled into my office chair and fired up the computer.

I clicked on a message that arrived this morning from D. Bowman.

> Hi Donna, Becky and I want to thank you for showing us your motel on Saturday. We are definitely interested and have some more questions for you. We need to know your gross profits for the last three years and your average utilities during the winter. Do you know whether we can build a pole barn on the property? Also, would it be possible to see it again next weekend sometime? My father and brother would like to see it and they'll be visiting us then. Call me anytime. I am including my work and cell phone

numbers, but if you call my office, don't tell them anything. They don't know I'm planning to leave. Hope to hear from you soon.

Don

Amazing, I thought. I had tried to sell that place for five years and had hardly had a bite. Now, it all seemed to be falling into place — the job at Pepper, the perfect house, and now maybe the sale of the motel. And Steve would be gone soon, no more fighting, no more stress. The thought of his impending death seemed unreal, although Dr. Alizadeh had made it pretty clear during the last visit.

"The chemo will just give you a little more time and will probably help with pain management," he said. "It will not cure you."

Even though it also made me feel guilty, I was anxious for all of the changes to happen. I knew the next few months, or however long it would be, would be very difficult.

***

A sort of routine emerged over the next several weeks. I would work all day most weekdays, except for Thursdays, which were chemo and doctor appointment days. Each week we would alternate visits to either the internist for insulin checks or to the oncologist for follow-up, then to the cancer clinic for an hour-long Gemzar (Gemcitabine) drip. Gemzar was a newer chemotherapy drug and was the drug of choice for the treatment of pancreatic cancer. The doctor had installed a port into Steve's chest so that he didn't have to face the poke of the IV needle each time. They'd just insert the needle into the port and he'd be on his way. He'd read magazines and eat the snacks that were left around for the patients. Steve would always choose a recliner with another empty one next to it and insist that I sit there next to him and hold his hand for a while. Thursdays were his best days. He had lots of attention and physically felt the best he would feel all week. After chemo, we'd normally go to a nice restaurant for a big juicy burger or a plate of Middle Eastern food. I tried to make sure Steve enjoyed the rest of the day, before the drug took effect. By midnight, he would be feeling terrible – nauseous, aching, and depressed.

The weekends were all bad. He'd lie around and refuse whatever I tried to feed him. He didn't want to go out of the apartment and he didn't want to be left home alone. He could hardly pet his dogs or watch the television.

By Monday night, he was a little better. He could usually eat something and he would want to watch television with me. He would sit in the recliner and drag my office chair so that it was beside him. He'd lift my legs and drape them across his lap. He'd act as though he cared about my comfort. Maybe he really did.

"Let's watch a movie," he'd say; "your choice."

I flipped through the channels and entirely by accident came upon a movie about a woman whose husband of 20 years decided he wasn't happy with their mundane life, and so left her for a much younger woman. I watched it much like a person watches an accident about to happen, not really wanting to, but unable to stop. The tears welled up in my eyes, then spilled over on my cheeks. The reaction was entirely involuntary and I tried hard at first to not make a sound. Not that it would have mattered anyway. I was not aware of any conscious thought, just the feel of wrenching, raw, agonizing emotion escaping my body. Eventually he noticed my tears and began wiping them from my cheeks.

"What's wrong?" he asked.

"Nothing," I said turning away.

"Talk to me," he pleaded.

"I've got nothing to say to you. It's all been said." I spat out the words. "It doesn't matter anyway. It's over!" I tried to push him away or get him to stop looking at me. I didn't want to talk about his betrayal. I was just beginning to put it behind us.

His concern, real or feigned, just made matters worse and soon the trickle became a faucet and the silence gave way to screams, wails and groans, and then I couldn't take a full breath. I sobbed and hiccupped and let out sounds I couldn't even describe. He cradled me. I struggled against his embrace. I tried composing myself, but something deep inside would not be quieted. There was nothing to do but surrender to the experience.

I had no sense of the passage of time, but the movie was over, and some comedian had taken over the screen. Steve was asleep in the recliner. I watched his chest rise and fall to be sure. My brain was numb but my body ached, like I had been doing manual labor. I didn't know it then, but this would be the last time I would be able to cry for years, maybe forever.

I got up and stumbled to the bathroom, flipping the switch as I passed through the bathroom door. "Holy Shit," I exclaimed, upon catching sight of myself in the mirror. My eyes were red and puffy from the brows to the cheeks. I had no whites. The outside corner of my right eye was entirely bloody. That'll be pretty in the morning, I thought. I began trying to come up with a plausible explanation because I couldn't afford to take off work until the eyes cleared up. Maybe a cold cloth would help.

***

The next two months were a blur. They were filled with paperwork and medical care. The closing of the home purchase was set for October 29, 2004, and the move from the apartment was scheduled for the next day. Don and Becky decided to buy the motel and because they couldn't get commercial financing based on the income it generated, I agreed to seller financing. We spent weeks negotiating the terms of the land contract and the timing of the transaction. I prepared for the trip to Maui to see my son Jeremy, who had moved there in June. I arranged trip cancellation insurance since it was anybody's guess whether Steve would be able to travel the first week of December. I continued to work every day although my work load had lightened. It was a good thing I had less work since Steve continued to receive chemo weekly until the third week of October. With all that was going on, there was no time for communicating with Matty. I assumed she had gotten on with her life as I had gotten on with mine.

Chapter Six

The Dying Days

It was October twenty-first – time for another blood test and a CT scan. Dr. Alezadeh wanted to see what good the chemo had done in order to determine whether to continue. The only appointment available at Beaumont was at 1:00 p.m., so it didn't make much sense to go to work. It took the better part of the day to get through the scan at the radiology department, and then we had to go to the cancer center to have blood drawn. Steve insisted on being pushed in a wheelchair. I could never tell if he was really feeling under the weather or if he was just being melodramatic, but I tried to be kind and supportive in case it was the former. The technicians wouldn't give a clue as to the results despite Steve's questioning.

"Doctor will give you the results," they all said.

After all the tests were completed, the receptionist alerted Dr. Alezadeh that Steve was ready to be seen. "Mr. DeVore," the young woman at the desk called out. I tried to conceal my irritation that after seeing him weekly for two months, they still didn't seem to get that he was deaf. If I hadn't been with him they probably would have kept calling his name until the end of the day before someone thought of asking him if they could help with something.

Through Steve I learned that it really is difficult to function in day-to-day social situations without being able to hear. Steve claimed he had been an activist in his younger days, lobbying for and achieving relay services for the deaf in Michigan. The first I had known of the existence of Michigan

Relay was when Steve and I first started dating, and I received a phone call from a woman saying "this is Operator 324 from the Michigan Relay Service with a call for Donna Lehl. Are you Donna Lehl?"

"Yes," I remember answering tentatively.

"Steve DeVore is calling you. Do you know how the relay service works?"

"No, not really," I said. "This is my first experience with it."

Operator 324 then described how the caller (Steve) was on a teletype machine, a TTY, and that he would type what he wanted to say and she would read his message over the phone to me. I would just talk normally and then the operator would type what I said so Steve could read it, and so on. While she was describing the process, she was also typing to Steve that she was explaining the relay service to me.

During our dating stage, before Steve moved in with me, we had had many long, very interesting conversations – Steve, the relay operator, and I. The relay operator would read Steve's words exactly as he typed them, or at least in theory. She would not preface her words to me with "he said . . ." So, there were occasions when some woman would be making suggestive remarks, telling me that she loved me, and couldn't wait to be with me again. Pretty weird, I recalled. But I had adjusted to this and pretty soon, it didn't seem so weird anymore.

"Mr. DeVore," the nurse repeated.

"Come on, babe," I said as I jumped up and began rolling the wheelchair through the wide wooden door to the medical suite. My words were lost on Steve since he wasn't looking at me, but like a lot of things I said to him in public, they were said not so much for his benefit as for mine, so that people would not wonder why I wasn't talking to him.

The young nurse led the way to one of the several patient examination rooms. She deposited a chart in the bin outside the door and told us the doctor would be with us shortly. I studied Steve's face and Steve studied the floor, or so it seemed, while we waited for Dr. Alezadeh. It was a little hard to call the slight young man with the impish grin "Doctor." He was about the age of my two children. But I suppose he had earned that title, I thought, as I waited for him to come through the door. We both really liked him. He was straightforward and yet he seemed unusually compassionate for a doctor. When Steve was in the hospital and Dr. Newman made his rounds while I was still at work, Dr. Alezadeh would come back a few hours later and talk to us together to make sure that we understood what Dr. Newman had told Steve earlier.

His grin was gone today. "How are you, Mr. DeVore?" he asked carefully, looking at Steve's eyes to be sure he was looking at his lips.

"Not good, doc," Steve said, extending his hand to the doctor.

"What's the trouble? Are you still having pain?" He asked as he took Steve's hand and shook it warmly.

It was clear that although Steve's speech had the odd sound I now recognized instantly as the speech of somebody who hadn't heard anyone else talking in their life, or in Steve's case, in five decades, Dr. Alezadeh understood what he said because he didn't look at me with that "what the hell did he say?" look.

"No, your drugs have me feeling no pain," he said with the flash of a smile. "But I know I'm dying. How long do I have, doc?" Steve's manner and tone were straightforward and unemotional, despite the subject. It seemed to me that maybe he didn't believe what he was saying and was just soliciting an argument against the statement.

The young doctor slid down the closed door until his butt was resting on his heels. The color seemed to drain from his face as he descended. It was clear he wasn't expecting the question, at least not yet. He glanced quickly at me, as if hoping I would say something that would somehow relieve him of the message he needed to deliver.

"I'm afraid the test results aren't good. The mass in the pancreas has grown during the course of chemo to four times its original size. Although the bile duct we opened is still intact, there's evidence of tumors in the kidney. The chemotherapy had no apparent effect upon the progression of the disease."

"So what do we do next?" Steve asked, appearing more concerned.

"There really isn't anything else that we can do for you except to make you comfortable," he said, looking straight at Steve, because he knew he had to in order for Steve to read his lips. I really admired this young doctor's courage and bedside manner.

"So, how long have I got?" Steve asked again.

"I can't say for sure how long you have," he spoke slowly, looking at Steve, "but most patients with inoperable pancreatic cancer expire within three to five months of diagnosis. On the other hand, we have been treating a woman here with the same condition for about a year and a half. All I can say to you is that you should do what you can to enjoy the time you have left and put your affairs in order. This disease will take your life."

The doctor's eyes trailed downward and his lips became obscured to his patient. Steve looked at me questioningly, so I would complete the sentence. After I signed to Steve "Cancer, die, you," he looked back at Dr. Alizadeh.

"Can you tell me how I will die – what it will be like, I mean?"

"No," Dr. Alizadeh started slowly. "There are different ways. Sometimes a patient will have a heart attack, or they will die of starvation or dehydration because they stop taking nourishment. Sometimes the lungs will stop working. But usually the patient won't know because they first become unconscious."

Dr. Alizadeh stood up and walked to Steve as he continued. "We'll do everything in our power to make sure that you don't feel any pain. If you feel any pain at all, just let someone know and we will do all we can to alleviate it." He took Steve's hand with his left hand while patting his shoulder with his right.

"Thanks doc, for your honesty," Steve said in a quiet, tired-sounding voice. "So what's next?"

"I could refer you to a hospice program. They can provide the palliative care and help with any other needs."

"Doctor, is there anything at all that can be done to treat this disease?" I asked, suspecting I already knew the answer.

"No, I'm sorry," he said speaking just to me at this point. More chemotherapy would just prolong the inevitable and you already know the discomfort caused by the chemo. Radiation is only effective when the cancer is localized. There is no surgical solution," his voice trailed off as if coming to the end of his checklist.

"Can I refer you to Beaumont's hospice program?"

"Yes, please," I answered. Steve seemed to be sleeping. He had closed his eyes and his head hung down. If he wasn't sleeping, he might as well have been since he was unaware of any conversation when his eyes were closed.

I gathered our belongings, pushed Steve's wheelchair through the office door, and stopped momentarily at the reception desk to see if they wanted to make Steve another appointment. They didn't.

"Hospice will coordinate all follow-up," said the receptionist as she reviewed Steve's orders. "But feel free to contact us if you have any questions."

***

So, that was it. He was released to die. I was kind of glad that Steve didn't feel like talking. What would we talk about? All the stuff we used to talk about didn't seem to really matter anymore and I needed some time to process what we'd just been told.

I pushed him to the lobby in front of the double automatic doors and after finding him a sunny spot, left him there without speaking. I went out the side manual doors and took my time going to get the car. When I returned to the loading zone, he was outside, looking expectantly toward the driveway coming from the parking lot. He had that "you left me and I'm scared" look that I'd seen in his eyes on many occasions over our 11 years together.

The first time was when we made our first trip to Bellaire together. We went to look at real estate before we found and I bought Surfside. We stayed at my ex-husband Ron's vacant house, but didn't sleep in his bed. That would have been too weird for even me. Eventually I became quite comfortable in the presence of both Steve and Ron. My family never quite got over their discomfort, but they joked about it, probably to relieve the stress.

"Here comes Donna Joy with her husband and her boyfriend" my father would say, trying to be comical.

Anyway, I got up early one Sunday morning when we were in Bellaire, and realizing that we had little to eat for breakfast, I went to the grocery store for eggs and bread. Steve was still sleeping so I slipped out, hoping to get to the store and back, and have some breakfast ready for him when he woke up. On the way back, I noticed a figure in the road between the highway and Ron's driveway. As I got closer, I recognized Steve. I pulled up alongside him and as he opened the car door, I was about to yell "what the hell are you doing on the road?" when I saw the frightened look on his face.

"I thought you left me here. I thought I'd have to walk

back home."

"What would make you think that? That's really crazy, I said making the ASL sign for "crazy," which just so happened was the same as the popular sign for crazy.

"Why would I just leave you 250 miles from home?"

He sort of hung his head and mumbled. And there were other times, such as when I went alone to visit my family and if I wasn't home as soon as I had planned to be, he would be pacing up and down in front of the motel. I would never know why he felt so insecure that he expected to be left without so much as a goodbye.

"Do you want to stop somewhere for dinner?" I asked when I knew he was looking at me. He didn't respond so I tapped my thumb and first two fingers against my lips; the sign for "eat." He shook his head. We rode home in silence, except for the music blaring from the radio.

I got him inside, took the dogs for a walk and when I returned, he was still sitting where I'd left him in his wheelchair, still wearing his jacket and cap.

"Are you hungry? Or would you like to take a nap first?" I said, after sitting in my office chair and pulling it knee to knee with Steve in his wheelchair.

He didn't answer, but a tear ran down his cheek, followed by another, then he was wailing. I put my arms around him and held him as he continued to cry audibly, shaking and soaking my shirt.

"It's okay. I'll stay here with you. I'll help you through it. They won't let you have any pain." I said for my own benefit since he couldn't see my lips moving.

"I'm so scared" was all he said.

***

The next couple of weeks went quickly because they

were full for me and seemingly uneventful for Steve. I went to work. Steve seemed comfortable, even happy when I returned home each evening. If it was sunny, he'd sit in the patio chair I bought him and let the dogs roam the length of their retractable leashes. He had an appetite now that the chemo was done.

We were both looking forward to our upcoming move. In the evenings, I packed and made arrangements for the closing and the move. My friends Hannah and Thad, and my brothers and sisters, and their families would all help. I rented a truck to move the stuff from the apartment. I choreographed the delivery of the new furniture we chose. We closed on the new home purchase on October 29th, and moved the next day. We were handing out candy to the Halloween beggars the following evening. Everything was falling into place.

The hospice nurses and the Rabbi began visiting Steve, but they had little contact with me, except for the pamphlets they left for me to read about making "arrangements" and dealing with loss. Steve occasionally felt well enough to plan and cook a meal as he had enjoyed doing throughout our time together. In the evenings we would watch television together, anything I wanted to watch, just as long as we sat together in the new reclining loveseat and held hands. It was kind of like the early days of our relationship, but without the steamy sex part. He was constantly saying "I love you" or making the ASL sign for I love you. I finally stopped saying "yeah right."

***

We decided to go to Surfside to pack and to move a load of the most useful items that remained there. We got up early Saturday morning and loaded the dogs and ourselves into the truck. I called Jane on the way up and made arrangements to meet her at the house for a little "packing party." Don and Becky made arrangements to come over and get a few maintenance tips from Steve, while he was still able to give them. The weather was unusually warm and sunny for the middle of November.

Steve slept most of the way to Tawas, which was not unusual, since the sun flickering between the leafless trees always had a sort of hypnotic effect upon him. He used to apologize for falling asleep as soon as we headed down the road, but it was entirely involuntary, he said. He was more wide awake when driving at night or on a really cloudy day. I had always let him drive at night since I was bothered by the oncoming headlights and was often overly tired by nightfall. In many ways we had had a very symbiotic driving relationship.

Once at Surfside, I busied myself with the tasks at hand and Steve sat down in his recliner and nodded off. I woke him twice and asked if I could help him out of his coat. He shook his head and clutched it tighter around his body. I only managed to get it off him when I convinced him to go to the bed that I had pre-heated with his electric mattress pad. He wouldn't eat; he only wanted to sleep.

Don and Becky came and went and Steve only managed to rise long enough to pose with them and me in front of the motel sign for a picture that Don would use to announce the change in ownership. Jane spent hours helping me pack. She wanted to talk with Steve and let him know that there weren't hard feelings over his verbal attack against her when she had "interfered" with an argument he and I had one day when Jane and I failed to come home when Steve expected us. He didn't give her a chance. He didn't even acknowledge her presence.

"Is he okay?"

"I think so," I said shrugging my shoulders. "I mean as right as someone in his condition gets. I think he's just tired from the trip and I put a new patch on him before we left. The fentynal seems to affect him more in the beginning and then gets weaker as it's delivered." I could see his chest rising and falling, so I knew he was still breathing. "He's been pretty good the last couple of weeks, since he quit the chemo."

I felt as though I was trying to convince myself that everything was all right.

On Sunday morning, I loaded the truck with furniture and utensils, then with the dogs and lastly, with Steve. He had done almost nothing and had eaten next to nothing all weekend. I was beginning to worry a little. I thought I would call his hospice nurse the next morning. He woke a couple of times during the return trip; once just about long enough to smile and squeeze my hand that was resting on the seat between us, and once when we were about 15 miles from home.

"Where are you going?" he asked, groggily. "You're going the wrong way," he said with a kind of urgency. He seemed kind of agitated. I was afraid he might grab for the steering wheel.

"We're going the right way," I reassured him. "We're on M-59. We're not far from home now."

It was hard to drive and look at him at the same time so he could read my lips, but I thought it was important to make him understand that I knew where I was going so he wouldn't try to do something rash. The dogs stirred in the backseat of the pickup and Kodi laid his head on the armrest between us. He nudged Steve's arm, but he was already asleep.

The rest of the trip was uneventful. I let the dogs out to run in their new backyard, and then woke Steve enough so that he would carry himself into the house with my help. I planted him on the loveseat, and then began unloading the truck. I was exhausted, but I knew that I was now on my own when it came to chores. He had tried to help me with them up until about a week ago when it seemed he'd suddenly lost interest in doing most things. I wasn't sure if he'd been taking more pain medicine than he should have, but then who could say how much was too much for someone in his condition. The doctors had told him not to suffer pain, not to worry about addiction to the strong painkillers and to do whatever pleased him. I didn't have that luxury; I had to do what needed to be done.

He dozed on and off until I tried to get him to eat something. He shook his head "no" and wobbled down the hall to the "sick" room. Someday this would be the guestroom, but for now, it held the hospital bed, a desk with Steve's computer on it, and it was decorated by the pictures and things we purchased together for a masculine den/sleeping space. There were the needlepoint prints of fish and lures, and the matching print that read "early to bed, early to rise; fish all day and make up lies" that had so amused Steve. There was the small wooden souvenir called "A Fisherman's Prayer" that prayed to be judged "good enough to keep" when the fisherman found himself in God's landing net.

He put himself to bed fully clothed, still wearing a jacket and his shoes. His breathing was raspy, but he'd always made a lot of noise when he slept because of his asthma and snoring. I used the time to finish unloading, to feed the animals, and eat a bit of dinner. I also needed to do a little laundry before the beginning of another workweek.

I heard him lumbering down the hall and recognized the sound of the cane in between his footsteps. Good, I thought, he won't fall, just before the THUD. When I got to the doorway of the bathroom, I saw him lying with his feet near the bottom of the toilet and the back of his head on the marble doorsill. His eyes were open and full of fear.

"Are you all right?" I asked him a little frantically. He only moaned and seemed to struggle, trying to lift himself from the floor. He couldn't even lift his head or arm from the cold white tile. He filled nearly the entire floor of the small bathroom. I couldn't even get into the room. I knew I couldn't sit on the floor with my "bad" hip because I likely wouldn't be able to get up. I bent over and began lifting him from under his arms, pulling his torso up, and propping it against my legs. Even though he had lost about 70 pounds in the past five months, I still couldn't lift his dead weight. After he had sat up for a few minutes and I had checked the back of his head to be sure he wasn't bleeding, he began to turn himself over onto his knees. Little by little, together we got him off the floor and standing in front of the toilet. I held him while he urinated and then walked with him back to the bedroom.

I helped him out of his clothing and into pajamas. I brought him his water bottle and his bedtime medicine. I wanted to ask him if he felt alright, but he looked solidly at the floor. I tried to lift his chin up so he would be looking at me, but he resisted. I bent sideways at my waist, trying to get below his face so that I could talk to him, but he wouldn't look at me. He was making sounds with his mouth, but I couldn't identify them. I noticed he was signing with his fingers, but I'd never learned to proficiently read finger spelling, unless it was done exaggeratingly slow and turned toward me as if I were looking at my own hands in the act of forming letters. Needless to say, no deaf person signed that way. I had no idea what he was saying to me.

I finally got him dressed and into bed. As soon as he dozed off, I left the room to get ready for bed. As I stepped out of the shower, I heard a THUD again, and the dogs were barking wildly in the hallway. I threw on a nightgown and opened the door to find Steve lying on his side in the narrow hall between the sick room and the bathroom. His cane was nowhere to be found.

"What the hell are you trying to do?" I yelled exasperatedly, knowing he couldn't hear me.

I ran to the coat closet, took out the wheelchair, opened it up, and put on its footrests. I took it down the hall and set the brake.

Over the next several minutes, together we got him off the floor and into the wheelchair. His head hung low, so I lifted his chin while pushing back on his forehead until I could see his eyes.

"Don't get out of the bed or the chair without me. I can't keep picking you up from the floor," I stated slowly so he could read my lips.

He made the sign for the letter P, ASL for "I need to pee." I rolled the wheelchair to the door of the bathroom, which was as far as it would go. This house was really not handicapped accessible, I thought, as I handed him his cane and put it into his right hand. I put his left hand on the counter and from behind, I tried to help him raise himself from the chair. He was a little unstable, but I quickly pulled the chair out of the doorway so I could get in behind him. With one hand on each side of his waist, I directed him to the toilet. He got himself ready, aimed, then nothing.

"Great" I grumbled into his back. "I bet he'll want to come back in a few minutes." I thought about the location of his "pee buddy," the urinal that he'd brought home from the hospital. He would be using that the rest of the night.

Eventually I got him back to bed, gave him some more pain medicine and as soon as he was asleep, I put myself to bed. It was 3 a.m. I went through my nightly mental routine – thanking God for my day, my family, my friends, considering what I had to do the next day at work, praying that Steve would pass peacefully when his time came. Just as I began to drift off into slumber-land, I heard another THUD.

At least this time he had fallen on the thick bedroom carpeting. "Why are you out of bed again?" I asked him while he was lying on his back near the hospital bed. "Do you have to use the bathroom?" Steve shook his fist up and down, yes in sign language. "How about using the pee buddy?" He shook his fist again. He helped me to get him up onto the edge of the bed. "Stay there." I ordered. "I'll be right back." I returned from the bathroom less than a minute later with the plastic urinal and helped him direct his penis into the opening. "I'll hold it for you. You just do your business," I said while contorting myself to get my face in front of his eyes which he was again directing toward the floor. I was not at all sure he read my lips.

Two or three minutes passed and I could no longer hear the sound of liquid splashing in the plastic bottle. He's got to be done, I thought. I took the bottle away and put it on the desk behind me. I tried to help him raise his pajama bottoms to cover himself, but he refused to let go of himself. He was pinching his penis so hard between his thumb and forefinger that it was flat like a piece of plastic tubing in a metal shut-off. I tried to get him to let go, but he held on tighter. I tried to get him to tell me what he was thinking, but he just kept mumbling. Eventually, I decided he was saying "stupider and stupider, you just get stupider and stupider." I assumed he meant me, but had no idea why I was suddenly so stupid.

Finally I managed to pry apart his fingers and when I did, I felt the warm spray of urine splashing on us both, soaking his pajama bottoms and running down his legs to the carpet. He looked up at me and said in the plainest English he had ever been capable of speaking: "I'm going to get someone to kill you."

As I cleaned him up, dressed him, put him back to bed, and dried up the puddle in the carpeting, I couldn't help but laugh. I could imagine him trying to arrange a hit on the Internet. He couldn't even take a leak by himself. Despite the harsh words, I wasn't too worried. He had become harmless.

By Tuesday morning it had been 48 hours since I had actually slept. He continued to get up every 15 or 20 minutes and raising the sides on the bed didn't help at all. He remained physically strong but totally unstable. He stopped speaking entirely, but his fingers flew in continuous sign language that I could not comprehend. The hospice nurse stopped by and was concerned about both of us. I desperately needed some rest and

Steve needed to be kept safe from falling. Together the nurse and I decided that Steve needed to go to the hospice wing of the hospital for a few days so his condition could be evaluated and so I could get a couple of nights of rest.

They came for him with an ambulance that night. He looked around furtively when they rolled him across the living room on the gurney and lifted him over the doorjamb. I felt alternating waves of guilt and relief. I followed the ambulance to the hospital, bringing some fresh pajamas and his glasses. I stayed long enough for them to assign him a room, administer his pain medication, and secure him in the bed. Then I kissed his cheek and went home to sleep.

***

For the next three days, I went to work, then went to the hospital until the end of visiting hours, and then went home to eat and sleep. He didn't speak to me during my visits, and after the second day, he really didn't look at me either. Mostly he slept and occasionally he struggled against the restraints they had begun using to keep him in bed after he'd gotten out of bed and had fallen before he got to the door of his room. I asked the hospice nurse if he would be all right if I went up north on the weekend to bring another load of stuff from the motel. The nurse advised me to stay in town.

My sister Darla decided to come and spend the night Friday and go with me to visit Steve in the hospital the next morning. She was shocked by the deterioration in his condition since she'd seen him at our brother Dana's wedding in September. He didn't appear to be conscious. He slept peacefully. She held his hand and stroked his forehead. After a little while, I suggested we go find some lunch. We stopped back in his room before heading across town and asked the nurse if he had been awake. She responded that he had not and then she asked Darla to step out of the room so she could check him.

As soon as Darla was out of the room, the nurse pulled off his bedding and lifted his gown, exposing a large adult diaper. She unfastened it and nonchalantly exposed his flaccid penis and shriveled testicles. I didn't recognize them. I turned away uncomfortably as the nurse replaced the wet diaper with a dry one and then put him and his bedding back together. The nurse told me that he hadn't eaten nor spoken since he'd been admitted, and that he had stayed put since his restless first day there. She said she didn't expect him to wake up and start talking, but advised me to talk with his doctor if I had other questions.

"Thanks anyway," I said. "I think we'll call it a day. I'll see you tomorrow. You know how to reach me if you need me."

The next morning, Darla went home and I picked up the newspaper from the front porch and returned to the hospital. When I entered his room, he did not stir. I kissed his cheek, squeezed his lifeless hand, and said good morning. Funny, I thought to myself, because if he was well he wouldn't have been able to hear my greeting. But he wasn't well, he was apparently unconscious. He breathed quietly for the first time since I had known him. I checked him a couple of times to be sure that he was breathing. He was, but in a very shallow, nearly motionless way. There really wasn't anything to do for him, so I read the newspaper and made a shopping list. I wondered if he would be coming home again, and if so, what he would want to eat. I felt guilty about leaving the dogs alone so much. I felt useless, restless. I really was not at all accustomed to just sitting around.

Finally, after killing time for about four hours, I decided to go grocery shopping, and then home. I would fill the evening by giving the dogs some attention, getting ready for another workweek, and watching a little TV.

***

I was sound asleep when the phone rang, but woke up and made it to the other side of the bed before the third and final ring. "Hello?"

"Mrs. DeVore?" an unfamiliar voice inquired.

"Yes," I answered, even though I was not. I had never changed my name to his, although he was annoyed by the fact and never tried to hide that annoyance.

"I'm sorry to have to tell you that your husband just passed away."

"When? I asked, feeling my knees buckling under me. Why didn't you call me sooner so I could have been there with him?"

"He passed sometime in the last half hour, but we didn't know it would happen now. He was okay at 11:00 o'clock when I checked on him and he died before I checked again at 11:30."

"Oh, okay," I said resignedly. "I'll be right there. It will probably take me about a half hour."

"Take your time," she said.

The hospice social worker had said to call anytime day or night and reassured me that she would be with me when the time came. I called, got voice mail, and left a message. Then I dressed, finger-combed my still wet hair, and grabbed a jacket as I said goodbye to the bewildered dogs. They must have been wondering what in the world was going on.

I knew where I was going since I had been there at least once a day for the last five days, but I didn't know what I was going for. It wasn't like there was anything I could do now. I didn't think his dead body was him, just the shell that held him during his time here. Maybe there were arrangements I needed to make. There were no tears. It was as though they were all shed in the days when we fought or maybe when I watched that movie that somewhat mimicked our situation. I hadn't cried since then. I hadn't even felt the urge to cry. Should I cry? Would I cry when confronted by his dead body?

I was amazed by how quickly I reached Dequindre when there was no traffic. Everyone else was at home resting up for another workweek. I would have to make burial arrangements when the morning came. I wondered who I should notify at the office. I didn't actually have any one person to whom I reported. I didn't want to call every partner in the department. I decided to call my assistant Shirley and let her notify everyone who needed to know, and then later in the day, I would send an e-mail to the partners and to Hannah with the burial details, and an estimate of the time I would be taking off.

The hospital parking lot was nearly empty. I remembered to use the emergency room door to get in after hours, and although it was a little longer walk, I didn't mind. I was in no hurry. I wondered if the hospice worker would meet me there as she had promised. The elevator opened on the second floor and I rounded the corner to the left, and then made a left again. His room was a few doors down from the nurse's station. It was absolutely silent as I walked tentatively down the hall and turned into his room.

His eyes were open, his mouth too, like a little bird – turned upward ready for some chewed-up worms. How odd, I thought. His eyes have been closed every time I've seen him since he was admitted here. Did he know it was the end? Did he open his eyes to see the light? Did he try to speak? I felt guilty that I hadn't been there with him and I also felt relief that I hadn't been there to see him draw his last breath.

I took his bony hand out from under the covers. It was still warm. I stroked his forehead and found it to be cool to the touch. I felt no urge to clutch his body or to cry. I felt his presence in the room, but not in the motionless body that had so let him down during these last several months. He seemed to be above and behind me. I felt like he was suddenly free. I was relieved that he did not have to suffer further pain or the embarrassment of others caring for his body. He would have so hated that.

I thought about who would miss him most – Kodi, his loyal little dog who was himself of advanced "dog years." He had been meeting me expectantly each day since Steve went to the hospital and often spent hours sleeping with his chin on the windowsill so he would be sure to see him when he came home, or so I imagined. He would be lost without him.

"Oh, I didn't realize anyone was here" said the middle-aged man in a khaki uniform who unexpectedly entered the room pushing a gurney. "I'll come back when you're done."

"I'm done," I said as I moved from Steve's bedside.

"Are you sure? I don't want to rush you."

"You're not rushing me. I need to get home and get some sleep. I have lots of things to do tomorrow, or rather later today," I corrected myself as I began the mental list of tasks that I needed to perform – call the rabbi, call the kids, call Delma (she would notify the rest of my family), call the office and let them know I wouldn't be in for a couple of days, e-mail Matty and Suzanna.

"Well, that was that. We wouldn't be growing old together after all," I thought as I gathered my belongings, and his plastic hospital sack full of the clothes he was wearing when he was admitted, and the extra pajamas I had brought him. I remembered the line from the Robert Browning poem we recited to each other in ASL and in spoken English at our wedding –"Grow old along with me! The best is yet to be, the last of life, for which the first was made."

It hadn't been long. It hadn't been the best in comparison to the early years with my children and lots of friends around. But this relationship must have been what I needed to reach the place I am headed. I don't believe in accidents. All things work together for good. I left the room and Steve behind. I found my way to the elevators and out of the hospital without seeing any of the nurses or the hospice worker who had promised to be there for me.

On the way home, I realized it had been at least a couple of months since Matty and I had communicated. I had been too busy I supposed, and she had probably moved on and really didn't want to talk anymore about her betrayal. I decided I would write her that night because my next few days would be very full.

From: Donna Lehl
Sent: Monday, November 22, 2004 1:08 AM
To: 'Matty '
Subject: Steven De Vore

Hi Matty,

Steve passed away a few hours ago, about 11:00 p.m. Eastern Standard Time on November 21, 2004. He died in the hospital, apparently in his sleep since he had not appeared to be conscious at all for the past several days.

I had to have him taken to the hospital last week when I could no longer handle him at home alone. He kept trying to get up, but he was not strong enough to stay up and I was not strong enough to hold him up or pick him up after he had fallen several times. I felt guilty about not keeping him home but I just needed a little rest after three days of constant monitoring. The last thing he ever said to me is "I'm going to have someone kill you." As awful as that sounds, it really was pretty funny since he was at that point totally unable to even care for himself, much less procure a hit man.

I still have not been successful in locating

either his mother or his sister to tell them. I will keep trying.

I will be having a Jewish burial in the cemetery he said he wanted to be buried in when he was first diagnosed. The rabbi who came to visit him through the hospice service said he could easily arrange it.

So, that's it Matty. I hope you are recovering from the hurt he caused and moving on in your life. I am. And I think I will be going to Maui next month to see my son after all. I think the change of scenery will do me good. We did move into the new house and after five years of trying, I have finally sold the motel. The closing will be in about three weeks. I have so much to do; I won't have time to feel sorry for myself.

Take good care of yourself and I do want to meet you if you ever come anywhere near Michigan. God bless Matty.

Love and Peace,
Donna

Conclusion

It was six o'clock on a Saturday morning and I was wide awake and dressed for the day. The coffee helped, but so did the fact that I had not slept soundly all night. I had played over and over in my mind what it would be like to meet Matty in person. I had seen pictures, but somehow I hoped that she would not be as attractive as she had appeared in them. It was bad enough that the other woman was younger and thin. I hoped there was something in which I would "score" more favorably. I shook my head in disbelief over my own shallowness. I really liked Matty. I would refrain from wishing her any ill.

Hannah would be here any minute and we'd be off. We planned to have breakfast sometime later on the road. It was about a four-hour ride and the plan was to pick up Matty and her friend from the Marriot Hotel near the airport about noon and take them downtown for lunch. We had planned about six hours to allow for breakfast, gas stops and the unexpected.

I checked myself in the mirror one last time as the doorbell chimed. Here we go, I thought. I was off to meet my dead husband's lover. Putting it that way, made it seem weird. But then I chuckled because there probably was no "not weird" way to think of the meeting. Thank God for Hannah. She didn't hesitate to agree to accompany me to Toronto. She only insisted on taking her Jeep so that her allergies would not be irritated by the dog hair that was imbedded in the upholstery of my car. We had come to refer to my Rav4 as the FURMBLE (fur-mobile) which was the vanity plate I planned to purchase one day.

Hannah drove across Ontario highways 401, 402, and 403 toward Toronto while I slept. Traffic was light on a Saturday morning and Hannah made it to the Toronto vicinity in record time. She woke me up to navigate to the hotel. Five miles out, I called the hotel and left a message for Matty that we would be there within fifteen minutes. Then after several wrong turns and corrections, we saw the Marriot ahead on the left, but somehow the road we were on did not take us there.

"I'm getting a little anxious," I said to Hannah as we both continued trying to figure out how to get where we wanted to go. "I don't know what I was thinking. Is this like the weirdest thing you've ever done?"

"No, not the weirdest, but right up there close to the top of the weirdest list." Hannah said, and then laughed.

"Okay, so the sign says 'Airport' to the left and the Marriot is real close to the airport. Oh, that's it – Dixon Road." I said as Hannah drifted toward the exit. "Watch out, there is a truck trying to pass you on the right," I advised while partially covering my eyes. "Thanks, I'd hate to get killed before I meet her."

We pulled into the Marriot parking lot about 11:45. "Okay, here we go. We're actually a little earlier than I told her we'd arrive. I think I'll find the restroom before I call her and tell her we're here."

We entered the expansive lobby in silence. I scoped the place for a likely spot for the public restrooms. While doing so, two women seated in a small sitting area caught my attention. "That's her," I said quietly to Hannah. I could feel my neck tighten. I'd have known her anywhere from the photos she sent me and from those I found on Steve's computer in the days following his death. She was tiny. She had dark brown hair, worn in sort of an old-fashioned up do. She was dressed casually in jeans and a red sweater over a white blouse. She wore bright red lipstick. The woman she was talking with seemed older.

Matty was facing the door, so when we walked in, she saw us immediately and when our eyes met, Matty stood up and took a few steps toward us. Her friend followed. The restroom would have to wait. I walked toward the women with Hannah bringing up the rear.

"Matty?"

"Donna?"

We exchanged greetings while simultaneously reaching out our hands to one another. It was immediately apparent that Matty was not accustomed to shaking hands. Her grasp was nearly non-existent in the vigorous handshake I had learned to deliver as a lawyer meeting and dealing with mostly men. Should I have hugged her? I thought. Somehow that seemed a bit too friendly for a first meeting even if we did know the most intimate information about one another.

"How was your trip?" Matty asked politely.

"Fine, uneventful. It only took a little over four hours to get here. How was your trip from Israel?"

"It was fine. We got here yesterday and we'll be here another two days visiting with friends before traveling to New York. Oh, I'm sorry," Matty said while wrapping her arm around her companion's shoulder, "this is my friend Elena. She decided to come along on my trip to America to be my chaperone," Matty said with a little laugh. Actually she has friends here as well, so we decided to take our vacations together and to visit them all."

"And this is my good friend, Hannah," I said gesturing toward Hannah. "We work together and she was kind enough to keep me company during the drive." Elena and Hannah exchanged the usual pleasantries. It was obvious we all felt a bit awkward and unsure about protocol for such a meeting.

"So where shall we lunch, here or should we go into downtown?" I asked the ladies.

We opted for the 20-minute trip to downtown Toronto

and followed the MapQuest directions to the Pickle Barrel Deli in the Centerpointe Mall. While we dined, we chatted about travel and our strange connection. We relived our first encounter and the pain that Matty and I each had suffered due to having loved the same man. We wondered whether he had ever loved either of us or whether we were each being used for some unknown purpose. We discussed the way that our friendships with other women and with our ex-husbands helped us heal. Within two hours, we seemed to be searching for things to talk about.

Matty looked at her watch and said, "oh goodness, it's time for us to get back to the hotel to meet up with our friends who are coming into town this evening." Thank God, I thought.

I knew this meant there was really nothing more that needed to be said. We quickly paid our bills, paused in front of the restaurant for a couple of photos, and headed back to the hotel, making small talk along the way. As we parted in the parking lot in front of the hotel, we promised to keep in touch, but I knew we wouldn't. What we had in common was gone. Steve was gone. The pain of the deception was gone. Our curiosity about one another was gone.

"I'm ready for a drink. How about you?" Hannah asked.

"Works for me. Where was that pub Thad told you we had to visit?"

Afterword

There was a blanket of freshly fallen snow on the ground as I rounded the sharp turn that divided the east and west sides of the cemetery where Steve had been buried. It was almost four years to the day that he took up residence in Section P at Hebrew Memorial Park, just behind the used car lot on Gratiot. I had only been there a handful of times since he was buried, but the last time I almost couldn't find his grave because the original small plastic marker had been weathered until his name was nearly invisible. I doubt that anyone else will ever visit his grave, I remembered thinking on that day, although it didn't seem right that it should go unmarked, as though no one had ever cared for him. I decided to reverse my original decision to save the money that a headstone would cost, and purchase a simple granite marker, something that would capture his essence.

I had to brush the snow from the stone, but there in the rarely bright November sun, it sparkled. I think he'd like it, I thought, as I admired the wolf he had emulated and the Hebrew words that represented the choice that he had made. It was perfect.

STEVEN RAY DEVORE
זאב בן אברהם
OCT. 26. 1946 - NOV. 21. 2004
ZE'EV

CPSIA information can be obtained at www.ICGtesting.com
Printed in the USA
BVOW030928090911

270774BV00006B/1/P

9 781608 300624